DON'T L SE YOUR HEAD

LIFE LESSONS FROM THE SIX EX-WIVES OF HENRY VIII

HARRIET MARSDEN

ULYSSES PRESS

This book is dedicated, with love, to my sister, Amy. Henry wouldn't have stood a chance.

Published in the United States by:
ULYSSES PRESS
PO Box 3440
Berkeley, CA 94703
www.ulyssespress.com

ISBN: 978-1-64604-129-9
Library of Congress Control Number: 2020947096

Printed in the United States by Versa Press
10 9 8 7 6 5 4 3 2 1

Acquisitions editor: Casie Vogel
Managing editor: Claire Chun
Editor: Pat Harris
Proofreader: Kate St.Clair
Front cover design: David Hastings
Interior design and layout: what!design @ whatweb.com
Artwork: shutterstock.com

This book is independently authored and published and is not affiliated in any way with the musical *Six*.

CONTENTS

FAMILY TREE

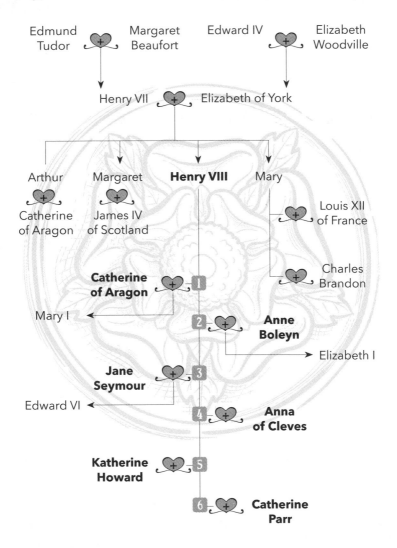

Edmund Tudor ♥ Margaret Beaufort

Edward IV ♥ Elizabeth Woodville

Henry VII ♥ Elizabeth of York

Arthur
♥
Catherine of Aragon

Margaret
♥
James IV of Scotland

Henry VIII

Mary
♥ Louis XII of France
♥ Charles Brandon

Catherine of Aragon ♥ 1

Mary I ←

2 ♥ **Anne Boleyn**
→ Elizabeth I

Jane Seymour ♥ 3

Edward VI ←

4 ♥ **Anna of Cleves**

Katherine Howard ♥ 5

6 ♥ **Catherine Parr**

FOREWORD

This book is called *Don't Lose Your Head*, but when you're married to Henry VIII, that's easier said than done. Divorced, beheaded, died, divorced, beheaded, survived. Six wives, each with her own background, education, religion, culture, talents, and hopes. Six queens in their own right, their rich lives exiled to the footnotes of history and dismissed in a nursery rhyme, remembered only for how one man chose to chuck them. Six women who were all, at one point, among the most powerful players at a most pivotal point of English history: a time when England became England.

Why do we remember them only as Henry's wives? He wasn't even the only husband. Catherine of Aragon, after all, was married to his brother first. Anne Boleyn and Katherine Howard were called "wife" long before they met Henry. Anna of Cleves lived a longer life as Henry's "beloved sister." For Catherine Parr, he was just one of four.

But all of them managed, for various degrees of time, to hold their own with a tyrant when it all went to hell. Each was tethered, willingly or not, to the most unbridled of beasts. How did they do it? How did Catherine of Aragon manage Henry's temperament for so long? How did Anne hold him off? How did Jane even compare? How did any of the later wives—Anna of Cleves, Katherine Howard, and

Catherine Parr—steel their nerve to get into bed with the world's most famous wife-killer?

Six women, with all their skills and all the courage they could muster, but not one of them came through unscathed. They didn't just have to be perfect Tudor women; they had to survive the worst of the Tudor men. A swollen boil of a bully by the end, a rotting slave to his appetites and hopelessly in thrall to his own ego. The greatest king in English history— or what we might now call toxic masculinity run amok. We'll never know what they might have thought, lying next to Henry at night as he sat up in bed and railed against the world. The only people who really knew were those in the room where it happened. And, because history is told by the victors, we've had only Henry's side. What would his wives tell us, if they could?

This is the story of all six wives, told in what I imagine to be their words, along with a few bits from Henry's mother and daughters. We twenty-first-century women live in an unimaginably different world, but the trials and tribulations of romantic relations remain much the same. The Tudors never had Tinder, but, by God, they got around. Passion, betrayal, boredom, desire, incompatibility, intellectual warfare, and plain old-fashioned lust—none of these are Tudor traits; they're the curse of the human condition. You might read this book and think, Jesus, it's better to be single. In which case, you'll love Anna of Cleves.

Henry VIII is a product of the women who came before him. He stands on the shoulders of giantesses. Of Empress Matilda—or Maud, as Alfred, Lord Tennyson, would see fit to describe her—the daughter of Henry I, arguably the first Queen of England. Of his mother, Elizabeth of York. His grandmother, the "Kingmaker," Margaret Beaufort. His own reign was made legitimate only by Catherine of Aragon's bloodline.

Even in Henry's time, when petty princelings vied for scraps and the great kings of Christendom threw their weight around in gold, women were holding court. Margaret of Austria, who ruled the Low Countries. Louise of Savoy, who took over ruling for Francis I while he was captive in Spain. Isabella I of Castile, Catherine of Aragon's mother, one of history's most impressive queens.

My own fascination with Tudor women began at a young age, when I first got hold of Philippa Gregory's 2001 novel, *The Other Boleyn Girl*. I'd only ever learned about Henry, you see. I'd never even heard of Mary Boleyn, nor imagined the pain and turmoil that it must have caused her, her sister Anne, their mistress Catherine of Aragon, and their contemporary Jane Seymour, to become entangled as they did.

This is not a history book, nor did I set out to write one. That said, I did read a lot of them. And in reading about women of the past, you learn almost as much about the men who wrote about them. As Christine de Pisan, a Venetian poet at the court of King Charles VI of France and arguably Europe's first professional female writer, joked in her highly influential *The Book of the City of Ladies* (1405), women must be inherently flawed because she "could scarcely find a moral work by any author which didn't devote some chapter or paragraph to attacking the female sex." "It was unlikely," she mused, "that so many learned men, who seemed to be endowed with such great intelligence and insight into all things, could possibly have lied on so many different occasions."

So the learned men who dismiss Katherine Howard as "wanton" or "flirtatious" ignore the fact that she was a teenage survivor of sexual abuse. The historians who buy into the notion that Henry risked foreign policy and ancient alliances because Anna of Cleves was plump and plain conveniently ignore the role Henry's ego played in rejecting her. I particularly enjoyed eminent scholar David Starkey's description of Henry as a "very good husband" and a good lover. I pray he writes my biography.

The way Anne Boleyn is portrayed is, of course, the most telling. Witch, whore, six-fingered temptress. Not: architect of religious reform. As Karen Lindsay posits in her excellent *Divorced, Beheaded, Survived: A Feminist Reinterpretation of the Wives of Henry VIII*, Henry's obsessive courtship of Anne now looks like sexual harassment in the workplace. Obviously, we shouldn't retroactively impose anachronistic

DON'T L*o*SE YOUR HEAD

social standards, but I think we can all agree that Anne said no for a very long time. It could have been a ploy, a seven-year game of hard-to-get, but I'm inclined to see it as something more complex. Bear in mind, she'd seen what being Henry's mistress had done to her sister's reputation. As Lindsay explains, Anne "had no social or legal recourse against the man who ruled the country. She continued, as so many women before and since have done, to dodge her pursuer's advances while sparing his feelings." Lindsay adds, somewhat euphemistically, "It didn't work."

So this book owes as much to the women of history as it does to the women who rewrote their histories. And, of course, to the writers of the musical *Six*, Toby Marlow and Lucy Moss.

The big triumph of the musical, and the challenge of this book, was in trying to divide the narrative into six. It's easy to forget that the women were all part of one another's stories. Catherine of Aragon, Anne Boleyn, and Jane Seymour all knew one another: they ate together, worked together, lived side by side. The stories of Anna of Cleves, Katherine Howard, and Catherine Parr overlap, too. You can't pull one thread without tugging at the whole tapestry.

The other big challenge was in trying to distill almost a century's worth of tumultuous history into one book. In 1536 alone, Henry managed to get through three wives: Catherine died not long before he disposed of Anne, who was barely cold in the ground before he married Jane. The Wars of the Roses, which put an end to the Middle Ages, all the way through the Renaissance and past the Reformation and into the Church of England, the Protestant reforms, Prince Edward's reign, and the death of Anna of Cleves…it could, and does, fill hundreds of books.

Then there's trying to untangle the Tudor who's who in a sea of Catherines, Annes, Henrys, and Thomases. That's to say nothing of all the different spellings: Catherine, Katherine, Cateryn…Henry really lucked out in having three wives who shared one name. I've gone with the spellings used in *Six*: Catherine of Aragon, Anna of Cleves (rather than the more commonly used Anne), Katherine Howard, and Catherine Parr. For consistency's sake, I've referred to Henry's children as Princess Mary, Princess Elizabeth, and Prince Edward, even though the girls lost that status more than once, and all three became monarchs eventually.

While I was writing this book, people kept asking me to pick my favorite queen. Honestly, I was as fickle as Henry. I began, as most do, fixated on Anne Boleyn: an extraordinarily powerful woman while still effectively an unmarried nobody. The woman who is remembered as a whore for what, exactly—her wits? Was Anne, with her shrewd mind and passion for the Church, not more responsible for the Reformation than Henry? She dazzled him for seven long years, until she got a sword to the neck for the great crime of being a real person as opposed to a fantasy.

I was, and remain, blown away by the courage and moral tenacity of Catherine of Aragon, who stuck to her guns and faced Henry down even though she doomed herself by doing so. It's easy to forget that she was queen alongside Henry for the best part of a quarter century: older, wiser, and better at ruling than he was. After all, most of what we think of as golden from Henry's reign is arguably her achievement. And had she been the eldest daughter in her family, we might remember her as a great ruler to follow her mother rather than as the unwanted first wife of a bigamist.

Katherine Howard gets a lot of my sympathy: a girl of barely seventeen when she was handed over like a toffee for the most powerful of murderers to chew on. A victim, if not of rape then certainly of abuse. An uneducated child who had grown up without any kind of family structure or discipline. None of Henry's wives got what they deserved, but least of all Kitty Howard, who died with her head on a stone block because she was brave enough to pursue her own desires: a boy she thought she loved.

I'd almost dismissed Jane "Boring" Seymour until I copped to just how much her hagiography affected my opinion. We all see her through the lens of sainthood that Henry posthumously imposed. Was she really so saintly, or even beloved? Or did she exist for him only as a damp counterbalance to Anne's fire? After all, as Gregory has Mary Boleyn tell her sister cheerfully: "We're all whores compared with Jane."

I have endless respect for the quiet nerve of Catherine Parr, Henry's final wife and the first woman ever to publish a book under her own name in England. In the turbulent last days of the Henrician court—with Henry's capriciousness, his violent temper, his murderous paranoia—that seems unfathomably reckless. The no-nonsense Northerner focused on her studies and survived her time with Henry to be reunited with the man she had always loved: Thomas Seymour, the brother of Jane. Of course, he repaid her by trying to sleep with her stepdaughter, but that's by the by.

But it was the overlooked Anna of Cleves who, in the end, stole the show for me. Too plain, too dull, too dumpy, was she? Anna of Cleves, the awkward German duckling who ended up living it large like a swan on a palace lake long after Henry and his last wife bit the dust. She had the ingenuity to negotiate her own freedom in a new country, with no friends, where she spoke no English, and come out on top. She's a testament to the fact that sometimes to succeed, all you have to do is survive.

INTRODUCTION

 ## A MOTHER'S LOVE

They say a mother-in-law is a pain but a daughter-in-law is a problem. Girl, try having six.

Mothers always think no woman can ever be good enough for their precious boy, but when your son is Henry VIII, King of England and Ireland, Supreme Head of the Church of England and Defender of the Faith, Father of the Royal Navy and flower of Christendom, the Golden Prince, the Tudor Lion…things are a little more complex. And when your son has stood as groom six times, you might start to wonder whether the problem is actually him.

What I hoped for was a daughter-in-law of royal blood and good breeding who would shore up the Tudor reign. A beautiful, intelligent, but humble woman who would rule by his side without taking over. Stylish, with good contacts. Accomplished and educated. A compassionate woman who would give alms to the poor. A helpmeet to run his household during the day and a lusty wench to satisfy him at night. And, in fairness, I got all of that. Just not at the same time.

Henry's story begins—as all men's do, from the loftiest of kings to the meanest of beggars—with his mother. It's the curse of the mother to feel guilty for the faults of her child. Although, in my case, a lot of the blame also lies with *my* mother-in-law. Plus, I feel I should point out that by the time Henry married his first wife, I was already dead.

My name is Elizabeth of York, wife to Henry VII, who was the son of the indomitable Margaret Beaufort. I was the first true queen of the Tudor reign, so I should know what a Tudor queen *really* needs to do to survive: produce a brace of sons. An heir, and a spare. Henry should know—he was my spare.

You see, Henry was never meant to be king. That honour belonged to Arthur, my firstborn. How history grinds on the knife-edge of the millstone. Learn this lesson, if nothing else: always have a backup plan.

But to understand how and why things went down the way they did with my son and his wives, and how he swelled from golden boy to bloated tyrant, you have to go back. Back before his birth, before mine. Before the Tudor dynasty. To a continent where flowers were just beginning to bloom on the graves of the Hundred Years' War.

You see, the royal House of Plantagenet, which had ruled the kingdom of England for three hundred years, was fighting the House of Valois for the right to the kingdom of France. Five generations; a hundred years; innumerable

DON'T LOSE YOUR HEAD

deaths. The longest conflict in European history. Some seriously strange twists in it, too, like little Joan of Arc, that maid of Orléans who they say saved France from the English. The young "saint" who apparently wore men's hose to protect her from rape—and who we charged with cross-dressing and burned three times. Go figure.

The English may have dominated at the Battle of Agincourt, but eventually the French gained the upper hand. That's the English way of saying, basically, "We lost."

The House of Plantagenet, which had originally come from France, lost the right to claim the throne. France lay in ruins, and England was riven from Europe forever, all of us under the shadow of the Black Death. But while France managed to get itself in shape pretty quickly, England stayed in turmoil. Who would take the English throne?

Picture the scene: the wet green fields of civil conflict. Two households, alike in indignity, vying for control of the land. Two rival branches of the House of Plantagenet: the House of York, with its white rose, and the House of Lancaster, with its red. Things get *very* complicated, with the Yorkists and the Lancastrians all basically interbred and mingled, but what you need to know is that eventually it would all erupt in another series of civil wars, called the Wars of the Roses, which eventually killed off the male lines of both. How men do hoist themselves on their own petards.

Enter the women, or, more specifically, one woman: Margaret Beaufort. The so-called Kingmaker. She was descended—down a somewhat illegitimate line, but don't let her hear you say that—from the Duke of Lancaster. Her mother was an early champion of girls' education, and Margaret could actually read and write, unusual for a girl growing up in the 1440s. And that was lucky for her, being a pawn in the Lancastrian courts.

In fact, she was even allowed to choose her own husband. Well, one of them, anyway. You see, Margaret was married off to John de la Pole, son of the Duke of Suffolk, when she was only a tiny child—maybe even an infant. But she never recognised the marriage—nor did canonical law, given that she was under twelve. When she was nine, she was offered Edmund Tudor, the half-brother of King Henry VI, instead. And she consented. Ambitious, even at such a young age. Or perhaps she was inspired by *her* mother-in-law, Queen Margaret of Anjou, who led the troops into battle with Richard of York and cut his head off.

And so on the eve of the Wars of the Roses, in 1455, Margaret was married off again at just twelve. Her husband, Edmund, was dead within a year, but he left her with his son in her belly: her only child, Henry Tudor—future King Henry VII.

Think about it: a young teenage girl, a widow, with the only child she would ever have, the heir to the English throne.

All her hopes, her chance of influence or remembrance or even of family, bundled in swaddling clothes.

Then Richard III, the last king from the House of York, seized the throne. And Margaret waited. She waited, and bided, and schemed, and plotted, and survived the death of another husband, because she knew what her son needed to get the throne that she believed should be his: a royal bride.

In this, she found an unlikely ally. Elizabeth Woodville, the wife of King Edward IV. Yorkists, no less! Take note, ladies. There's no reason not to work with bitches if it gets you what you want. And she was something of a celebrity, given that Edward IV had married her for love despite her lack of swag. Quite the scandal in those days. In fact, Edward IV was the first English king since the Norman Conquest to marry one of his own people. So she was a *very* big deal.

Even though Richard had snatched the throne, he was too insecure, too petty, too weak to truly lead. He saw Elizabeth and her brood of royal children as a threat. He took her sons, his sort-of nephews, those poor little princes, into the Tower of London, and they never came out. After 1483, nobody saw them again.

But Richard made the mistake that so many men had made before and many more were still to make: he overlooked the daughters. An eldest girl with a strong claim to the throne on her own merit. Heiress to the House of York. That girl was me. Everyone said I might have to marry him after his wife, Anne Neville, died, but I put my foot down.

So my mother and Margaret banded together in a world of men. My mother, suffering the terrible loss of her sons, and Margaret, clinging to the son she had borne when she was just a child herself. The Lancaster heir to Henry VI, and me, the York heir to Edward IV. The two scheming biddies thought to unite the bloodlines through their children. Richard didn't see it coming. Woe betide the men who underestimate the mothers. And so, we promised to marry.

And when Henry Tudor grew up and scrambled a victory against Richard at the Battle of Bosworth Field, the last big battle of the Wars of the Roses, he became king by default: Henry VII. He kept his promise to me, and we were married a few months later. He the red rose of Lancaster, I the white rose of York. Together we were the red-and-white Tudor rose. And so you have it. Margaret Beaufort had united the houses through sheer force of will. She basically invented the Tudor dynasty.

She was also a *giant* pain in the arse.

By the time my Henry got his throne, she was so used to running the show that she carried on long after I became queen. She dictated everything, literally wrote the book on Tudor birth and death rituals. She ruled the court like a horse-master with a whip. I can still picture her now, in her scratchy, pious hair shirt, passing judgment on me as a wife and as a queen.

"Listen to me, girl. Your life must *appear* a pursuit of leisure. Accompany the king at hunting, carry his favour at the joust, exclaim with delight at the stupid masquerades, eat like a bird at the picnics, and dance like a courtesan at the balls. You must take Mass with piety and listen to sermons with interest. Fake it, if you have to.

"You must learn embroidery, music, card playing, and just a little flirtation. Only flirtation, mind you. It is a desirable Tudor woman who knows enough about courtly love to parry a witty badinage. It is less desirable to appear as if you have firsthand experience.

"But to be a good Tudor queen is more than being a good wife. It's a full-time job. You are responsible for the queen's rooms and your own court of hundreds, from the master of the horse down to the lowest servants. You have to set an example of good queenly behaviour to your ladies-in-waiting and the young maids. Teach them to read—it's a good way to keep young ladies' minds off the courtiers. Organise the household, and keep a smile on your face. You will learn statehood and regency in case your support is ever needed.

"And, most importantly, you must never, ever complain. You will suffer the poisonous lead in your makeup, the tight stomachers on your gowns, the heavy hoods on your head, and the urine to lighten your hair. You'll wear heels you can't walk in, wear a corset you can't breathe in, and embroider clothes you can't wear. You will satisfy your husband unreservedly and look the other way when he takes lovers. You'll probably die trying to bear his children.

"No back talk. No slovenly behaviour or unseemly innuendo. No moaning. No demanding. No overeating. No embarrassing the family. And, above all, don't lose your head and forget your place."

On and on she went until my head was dizzy with it. A long list of nos in her guide for how to be the perfect daughter-in-law. I swore never to tell my son no.

So, yeah, my mother-in-law was a pain. I had hoped to outlive that wizened old crone, but to no avail. Although I will say, she did a lot of good. She teamed up with scholars and studied religion. She set up two readerships in divinity at Cambridge, which gave anyone the right to read religious works. You have to hand it to her, really. In fact, I named my first daughter after her: Margaret, who would later marry James IV of Scotland and become regent after his death. The Scottish Queen, if you will. My youngest daughter, Mary, came along in 1496, and despite being married to the old King Louis XII of France for only a few months, she would always be known as the French Queen.

And what of my husband, now King Henry VII? A soldier of fortune, a merchant of commerce, a wily courtier, and a man whose rod of iron will bent only for his mother. My husband had too recently plucked his crown from the mud of a battlefield to be sure of it on his head. He ruled over an austere, careful court. He was pretty stingy, actually, although, looking back on it, I realize he had every right to be, given that he had inherited a nation utterly bankrupted by the civil wars. Still, it pissed him off when I gave too much to charity.

You needed to know all of this to know how and why we raised our firstborn, Arthur, named for the legendary king of Camelot. The Prince of Wales, born in our first year of marriage. The blessing on the start of our golden age, the hope of the House of Tudor. Arthur was raised to rule, and rule well. Margaret, Henry, and I all wanted to make his reign safe. He was educated in geography, biology, and not a little history. He studied literature and politics, treatises and treaties. He was taught to be careful with money and humble to his God. Respectful to his elders and pleasant to his lessers. He felt the weight of responsibility on his tiny head from the moment he was born. What a king he might have made.

And then we had our spare: Henry—or Harry, as we called him when he was a child. A bouncing baby who I couldn't bear to scold. A towheaded imp who just wanted to have fun. Energetic, charismatic, intellectual but not overly studious, generous to a fault, and handsome as a devil. And we never thought to discipline him. We never thought we needed to. We could never have known that my indulgence and his father's indifference would curdle like milk to indigestion and that his impulsiveness would grow to tyranny.

So when we lost Arthur, we turned to Harry. And Harry became Henry, and there was nothing any of us could do. Because we'd never told him no. And that's how he ended up choosing his dead brother's widow for his wife. I reckon that's why he ended up with six. But that's not my story to tell.

Plus, I think you'll agree, he was quite a catch in his prime…

DON'T LOSE YOUR HEAD

PROFILE

NAME: Henry VIII, King of England; formerly Harry, Duke of York

OTHER TITLES: King of England and France, Lord of Ireland, Supreme Head of the Church of England, Father of the Royal Navy, Defender of the Faith

BORN: 28 June 1491, at the Palace of Placentia in Greenwich, Kent

PARENTS: Henry VII and Elizabeth of York

NOTABLE ANCESTORS: Edward III (illegitimately)

SIBLINGS: Arthur (born 1486), Margaret (born 1489), Mary (born 1496)

LOOKS: Tall, blondish-red hair, blue eyes, fair skin, pouty mouth, strong calves, rotund stomach

PERSONALITY: Extravagant, impulsive, spoilt, generous, demanding, intelligent, fickle, insecure

INTERESTS: Music, religion, hunting, feasting, tennis, jousting, gambling, building ships; later, political executions, building of expensive palaces, sex, the divine right of kings

EDUCATION: Highly educated and fluent in English, French, and Latin; well versed in Bible studies and religious schools of thought; into reading and writing books

RELIGION: Started off Catholic; after that is anyone's guess

MARRIAGES: Six, plus at least two full-blown mistresses and numerous affairs

MOTTO: *"Coeur loyal"* ("Loyal heart")

CROWNED: 24 June 1509

CHAPTER 1

CATHERINE OF ARAGON

PROFILE

NAME: Catherine of Aragon, also spelled Katherine or Katharine, known as Catalina, La Infanta

OTHER TITLES: Princess of Wales (when married to Arthur); Dowager Princess (when Arthur died); Regent of England (when Henry fought in France, June 1513); called Governor of the Realm and Captain General

BORN: 16 December 1485, at the palace Alcalá de Henares near Madrid, Spain

PARENTS: Isabella I of Castile and Ferdinand II of Aragon

NOTABLE ANCESTORS: Catherine of Lancaster and Edward III

SIBLINGS: Isabella (born 1470), Juan (born 1478), Juana (born 1479), Maria (born 1482)

CHILDHOOD: Infancy on her parents' military campaign against the Moors in Spain, betrothed at three, and raised in the Alhambra palace in Granada

LOOKS: Red hair, blue eyes, fair skin, very petite

PERSONALITY: Intelligent, religious, compassionate, strong-willed but regal

EDUCATION: Highly educated; could read and write in Spanish and Latin; spoke French, Greek, and English; a student of theology and philosophy; a lover of literature

RELIGION: Roman Catholic, a member of the Third Order of Saint Francis

MARRIAGES:

- Arthur, Prince of Wales (elder brother of Henry VIII), November 1501 at Old St. Paul's Cathedral, age 16; widowed in 1502
- Henry VIII: 11 June 1509 at the Church of Observant Friars outside Greenwich Palace, age 23

AGE DIFFERENCE WITH HENRY: Five years older

MOTTO: "Humble and loyal"

CROWNED: 24 June 1509 with Henry in Westminster Abbey

CHILDREN: Six, one surviving

- 31 January 1510: a stillborn girl
- 1 January 1511: a boy, Henry, Duke of Cornwall (died 22 February)
- 17 September 1513: a boy who died shortly after birth
- November 1514: a boy who died shortly after birth
- 18 February 1516: a girl, Princess Mary (later Lady Mary and Queen Mary I)
- November 1518: a girl who died shortly after birth

MARRIAGE WITH HENRY ENDED: 23 May 1533, after twenty-four years, when it was ruled unlawful; Henry claimed that her marriage with his brother had been consummated, and the Bible forbids a man to marry his brother's widow—even though the pair had papal dispensation

DIED: 7 January 1536 at Kimbolton Castle, probably of cancer

BURIED: Peterborough Cathedral

DID YOU KNOW?

- I was the only one of Henry's wives older than him.

- Some people said I had a stronger claim to the throne than Henry's father, on my mother's side. Not everyone in Europe accepted the Tudor reign as legit, so Henry needed me to validate their line.

- In 1507, I became the first female ambassador in European history when I represented Spain at the English court.

- I brought the first recorded Africans to London, in my retinue of servants from Spain.

The first thing you need to know about me is that I was never divorced. When Henry lost his head over that French-tongued *puta* and tried to claim that our marriage had never been real, the Pope said no. I think that was the first time anybody ever tried that with Henry. So my husband defied *El Papa* and took control of the Church. He broke with Rome, he broke with ancient allies, and he broke with his God. Bit of an overreaction.

Dios mío, I can joke now, but it wasn't funny then. The horror of the dissolution, even after all these centuries. The blood spilled, the heretics burned. The monks cast out, and the pilgrims left with nowhere to pray. The statues of the Virgin Mary with their heads knocked off like common whores. The great religious houses turned over to grasping upstarts. The rivers of ill-gotten gains. And the England that we'd built together, that his dead father had imagined and his dead brother had begun, torn from Europe like a calf mewling for a teat.

Henry lost the respect of his court and the trust of his people, and gave up his spot in the afterlife next to me, and for what? Sex?

Well, so you might have heard.

The truth is, it's never *really* about sex. It wasn't even about her, in the end. It was about ego, about control, about wanting what he wanted and being willing to smash everything for it. Like a horny Hulk. Thousands of years of unity shattered like a looking glass. She just gave him the guts to do it. But God knows, the cracks had appeared long before Anne Boleyn.

Everybody remembers her, the wife who turned his head before she lost hers. She changed history, they said. Fewer remember me, the wife he turned from. But I ruled alongside him, with him, *for* him, for twenty-four years. A quarter of a century. The golden era of Henry VIII, when he was still a virile young prince and not a bloated buffoon. A thankless task, being a Tudor wife. A selfish man will always throw it back in your face when he doesn't get what he wants. And what he didn't get from me was a living son. But he didn't get it from her, either.

So Henry went back on the papal dispensation that had allowed us to marry, and he had our marriage annulled. That left him a single man and me the widow of his elder brother. The Dowager Princess of Wales, no less. But he never divorced me.

My name is Catherine of Aragon—the most relevant Catherine in this story, *ya tú sabes*—but it wasn't always. I used to be called Catalina, La Infanta of Spain. Beloved youngest child to a powerhouse mother, who had already provided the all-important heir, my brother, Juan, plus a useful bevy of daughters to be traded in marriage. The youngest of five, a girl, I existed only insofar as I might grow up to marry someone useful. But I looked like an English child, with the fair auburn hair and blue eyes of a country maid. Never conniving, but I always knew the value of a wide-eyed smile from a petite girl.

My mother was Isabella I, ruler of Castile, a kingdom in the sun-scorched southwest of what you'd now call Spain. My father, Ferdinand II, was King of Aragon, the fertile green valleys of the east. They brought together the kingdoms and, with their marriage, became the first King and Queen of Spain. My mother, the holy warrior, with her crusading will to deliver the word of God and light of the true faith and to drive the Moors from the hills. My father, the merchant schemer, with his shrewd wiles to bend the little boys of Europe to his dream of a united Christendom, adored by Niccolò Machiavelli and dominated by his (slightly older) queen. Lovers, allies, co-rulers, with both of their heads on the coin. I planned to follow in my mother's footsteps.

I spent my infancy bouncing along with my parents' military campaigns against the Moors. The year after I was born, my mother trapped them in Granada like rats in a sewer. I was there at the siege and at the surrender. To the victor go the spoils, and what spoils they were. During most of my childhood, I was stretched like a cat in the gentle shade of the Alhambra palace, the most beautiful

DON'T LOSE YOUR HEAD

ever built. Never underestimate the power of heresy on architecture. The Moors might have been unbelievers, but they certainly weren't savages. I was lulled to sleep by the music of trickling water and danced in floating silk through the patches of sun in the stone-baked courtyards. Servants anointed me with precious oils, and I lived, in fabulous isolation, in the safe embrace of women.

Apart from my strict tutor, who schooled me unmercifully in history, theology, and classical literature, everybody loved me. I was *La Infanta*, the beautiful child polished to within an inch of perfection with education and languages and skills in dance and embroidery. If I'd known then that I was going to give that all up for a lifetime of wet English winters and male ego, I'd have shat a brick.

My parents forged a country as a blacksmith forges a sword, drove out the Moors and Jews, and paid the Italian wanderer Cristóbal Colón to bring us back the New World— you might know him as Christopher Columbus. They were a force to be reckoned with, a force far greater than the puny little plop in the sea known as England. But my father decided there might be a better use for me than oils on the buttocks. An alliance with England, he thought, could help muzzle the French dog between the two. And that's how I, a royal Princess of the Blood and child of the Conquerors, was promised to Arthur, Prince of Wales. Future wife of the King of England. It's funny; I probably had a better claim to the throne than he did.

King Henry VII needed me and my blood, trickling all the way down from John of Gaunt and out between my legs, to validate his own reign, so that his son could have truly royal children. He was actually my third cousin, although he came down the illegitimate line. Not everyone was on board with the Tudors, and Henry VII needed some insurance.

Plus, he needed Spanish gold. And if it hadn't been for the greed of that commoner, that tightfisted raven grasping for a dowry worthy of the king he wished his prince to become, we might have all gotten along a little better. Money and families mix like mead and piss. When you commoditize a girl like that, weigh her in jewels and plates and stick a price tag on her, you sacrifice her on the altar of other men's greed. And so, at just three years of age, I was sold to a foreign princeling for two hundred thousand crowns. Half up front, half to come after my wedding.

Arthur married me by proxy when I was fourteen and he was thirteen. I wasn't even in the room where it happened. And two years later, with much pomp and pizzazz, I would be sent to a country I'd never seen and a boy I'd never met. Perfumed with Castilian sophistication and intellectual arrogance, I was traded like a camel in a desert to lie under a milksop younger than me. All to be Queen of England. That was my first lesson in what it means to be queen. Don't let dignity get in the way of destiny.

After a two-year courtship of letters in Latin, dictated under duress by our tutors and parents, I left the coast from La Coruña and headed with my back to the open blue as I watched my homeland recede into the horizon. I never saw Spain again.

Ay, pero what a journey. Hercules had his labours, and I had mine, crossing through every storm Poseidon could throw at us. Stomachs rolling, faces lashed with sea spray, my best friend, María de Salinas, and I clung to the lilting wood of the ship, scolded by our *duenna*, Doña Elvira, as we squawked with fear. I shouted to María: "No mortal has ever been so cold and wet as this!" Of course, that was before I ever went to Wales.

But finally, on 2 October we landed on a rock in Plymouth. And that was where it all turned around. What a welcome.

What a parade! I was dazzled with the attention. I don't know who the English were more fascinated with—me, the exotic pomegranate for their beloved prince, a vision of mantilla lace—or the African servants I'd brought in my retinue. A guard of honour took me on the road between quaint towns dotted between verdant hills, and as the English people sang my welcome I began to love my new home. I had left Catalina of Spain; I had arrived Princess Catherine.

My new father-in-law, however, was lacking in the grace or courtesy he might have acquired through legitimacy. He deigned not to meet me as planned at Richmond Palace, a spectacular and worthy setting just outside London to rival Alcalá, the palace of my birth near Madrid. Instead, he gathered up his ragtag band of soldiers he called courtiers to gallop through the mud and surprise us in Bath. Men, take note. Women rarely appreciate that kind of surprise.

I had been raised in the Spanish harem, in isolation. So when he demanded to be admitted to my chamber just to get a look at me, as if I were something he'd buy in a market, it should really have been a tip-off about this island, with more delusions of grandeur than hard cash to burn. I rolled out of my bed in nothing but a shift to face him and meet my new husband. But I stood my ground and fell back on my dignity. I don't think he saw that coming. But you do not claim superiority if you stoop to lower standards. Head up,

DON'T LOSE YOUR HEAD

chest out, grit your teeth, and keep your cool. Even when an old lecher is blatantly staring at your breasts.

Before Arthur and I met in person, the letters we'd exchanged were dutiful—"my dearest spouse" and all that tripe. But don't make the mistake of thinking you know a man just because you've been corresponding for what seems like years. He might have written to me in perfect scholarly Latin, but it was only when we came face-to-face that I realised his accent wasn't worth *nada*. My first insight into male-female relations.

I said to María: "How is it that we're speaking the same language, but I don't have a clue what he's saying?" She looked at me as if I were *loco* and said: "But won't he learn Spanish?"

(Spoiler alert: he did not.)

I looked at the pale, weak boy peeking from behind his father, enthralled and unsure, and I thought to myself: "This boy needs me to act the queen if he is to become king."

Henry VII was satisfied. Arthur was satisfied. And I swallowed my pride and got to work. I think it might have been the first time in history that two people have ever compromised by speaking French. And when we rode up the cobbles into London for our wedding, the city went wild. All these years later, I can still hear the bells echoing in my ears that moment when I thought, It's all been worth it. My triumph:

when La Infanta of Spain became Princess of Wales. That day, I married Arthur.

And that was the day that I met his brother, Henry.

Or Harry, as we knew him then. Just ten years old and already stealing the spotlight. On his own brother's wedding day, no less. Harry was everywhere, dancing, singing, flinging himself about in his shirtsleeves. I was fixated on Arthur, my new husband, and amused watching the heir try to maintain his dignity while the spare cavorted like a jester. I thought that Harry might be a handful, for sure. I was too dazzled by the scale of St. Paul's Cathedral and too tin-eared from the noise in the streets to pay much attention. But someone up there was laughing when little Harry grabbed my arm and marched me into the cathedral and up an airborne bridge they had built from the door to the altar.

And so, Arthur and I were married. And we were put to bed by the court. I was prepared by my *duenna* to be impaled— or lightly poked—by my new husband.

But we were just children. They forced us together like animals to breed, but we didn't even speak the same language. I spent my wedding night in his arms, but he never made me his wife. All that fancy schooling and he couldn't fathom a hymen. Go figure.

What, you think I'd change my story after all this time? I went to my grave swearing that Arthur had never consummated our marriage. Half a millennium more isn't going to break me. That's my story, and I'm still sticking to it. Truth be told, I wasn't as worried as he obviously was. There's none so sensitive as a man who can't get it up. Best thing you can do is move on, because they will *not* appreciate your pity. Besides, I thought we'd have years to get it right.

They did things differently in England, I soon learned. Men mingled with women in the queen's rooms. There was jousting and feasting and terrible food. And the *smell* of these people. I'm fairly sure no Tudor ever washed. They just perfumed their heavy velvet clothes. They didn't wash those, either. They didn't even drink the water, much less bathe in it.

My new mother-in-law embraced me as a daughter, but she was queen in name only. Arthur's grandmother, My Lady the King's Mother, Margaret Beaufort, was an old battle-ax, and no mistake. I watched, curiously, as she ruled the court through her son.

I hid behind my two new sisters, Margaret and Mary— promised to Scotland and France, future queens both. I struggled to learn English, a flat barbarian's tongue, with none of the flavour of my native Spanish or fluent French. But I was cautiously happy.

Until they sent me to Wales.

It pains me to admit this, after almost a lifetime in England and twenty-four years as ruler, privy to the most nitty of gritty details; but at the time, I'd no sense of the geography. I came from the deserts and mountains and drama of Spain and all its distinct kingdoms. I'd pictured England as a flat little mudhole bordered to the north by savage Scots, their version of our Moors.

And I was more or less right. Except for Wales.

Wales seemed to think it was its own country. It was certainly in love with its own Welshness. It practically *ejaculated* in Welsh. But the son of the King of England is also the Prince of Wales, and so Arthur and I, the "newlyweds," were shipped off to the dark borderlands of Welsh fervour. Arthur needed to learn the art of kingship, and I needed to learn to bear discomfort in that squat little town hall they called Ludlow Castle.

My memory of Wales is blurry: fragments of a language that sounded like a madman speaking in tongues, a culture I couldn't understand, and a dark, draughty hellhole in which I couldn't get warm. Far from both my old family and my new, with Arthur too overwhelmed with princely duties to do the one thing he was supposed to do: me.

Who knows how long things might have gone on like that there, but then everything changed when the sweating sickness came.

This was my first experience of that uniquely English disease, which hovered like the sword of Damocles above my new home each summer and winter. A strange illness that could strike a man down like a whip but to which the rest of Europe seemed immune. A curse, some said, on the Tudor reign. And when the sickness came to Ludlow like a deadly fog, my Arthur was dead within days.

My prince, the future king, the best of the Tudors, died twisting in his bedsheets and drowning in his own skin. We hadn't been married for even six months. And I was a worthless widow.

Well, not quite. The second half of the dowry was still owed, after all. I was worth precisely one hundred thousand gold ducats. But although he was reeling from the death of his firstborn son, Henry VII had no intention of losing the rest of my dowry just because I had lost my husband. And my father had no intention of paying it.

And so I waited. And I waited. I stayed frozen in my grief and disappointment. The Spanish on one side and my father-in-law on the other, locked in a battle for which my body was the field. A stalemate in which nobody wanted responsibility for me.

And then my poor mother-in-law died. The White Rose of York died trying to give her husband another baby, at the age of thirty-seven. So soon after the wound of Arthur's death, Henry VII lost his wife and baby.

So you'll forgive me for not having seen it coming, what happened next. Henry VII's eyes fell on me. His wife and children barely worm food and he's looking for a place to spend the night. Never underestimate the twin powers of lust and frugality. Thank God my mother put a stop to it.

But it made sense for *someone* to marry me, considering how much I'd cost. And I still had the same value as a bride. Sort of. Luckily, there was another contender. Harry, the new Duke of Cornwall and heir to the throne of England. And so, in June 1503, we signed a binding marriage treaty.

And I waited some more. All those long seasons, my most fertile years, I waited. I could have whimpered at the cold, the damp, the lack of *elegancia*. The dark stagnancy of it all. The heavy velvet and musty damask gowns. The loneliness. The wet green gardens, when I had once ridden the hills around the Alhambra. I, a child of crusaders, was forced to turn like a child at a dance class around a lawn. And the food! No salad, no fresh fruit, not a vegetable in sight, just cured meats and pies and endless small ale. But I kept saying to myself, to do its job a privy must learn to take shit.

I didn't realise it then, but we'd shamed Henry VII by rejecting his proposal, by showing him for the sad old man he was. He had to punish me. He had Harry stand up in front of his council and swear that he had been too young to be betrothed. I mean, he had been fourteen.

My mother died the following November. It sounds stupid, but I could barely comprehend a world without that kind of spirit. Although, during my time in England, she'd disappointed me as a mother. She treated me less like a child and more like a wayward ambassador. She and my father left me to rot for the purposes of politics. But once she died, my value fell even further.

I nearly starved, you know. Literally. A princess left with nothing to pay her servants or to buy food. The Earl of Derby wanted to marry my precious María, but I had to look my best friend in the eye and tell her I had no promised dowry to give her. The shame, and the quiet relief. My clothes were worn down to threads. I was forced to sell my golden plate just so we could eat. My people were depending on me, and I was all alone.

To get around it all, my father made me the Spanish ambassador at court, which gave me not only an allowance but also a position that forced my father-in-law to meet with me. The first female ambassador in European history. Out of great suffering can come great professional opportunity.

But they hung on to my dowry as if it were the only gold that England ever needed. But in 1509, seven years after my husband died, so did Henry VII. The last obstacle. And Harry stepped into the spotlight—and still wanted me.

Bear in mind, I wasn't just the beautiful older woman he'd lusted after for most of his puberty. His first sight of me was as a bride to his elder brother. He was always jealous of Arthur, the true heir. Whatever toy Arthur had, he had to have. I was the toy that he'd always wanted and whom the elders had kept out of his reach. He had to have me.

It was practically the first thing he did, as a young man of eighteen bounding up to the throne. And besides, it was still a good match. I was royal, I was pretty, I was a worthy ruler, the English people still loved me. But like all boys with toys, he would grow tired of me eventually.

So why did I agree to it? *Mierda*, did you just ask me that? To be the new Queen of England, married to the handsome young star of Christendom, the most powerful woman in Europe? To have a chance to rule like my mother, to mould Henry into the king I thought he could become? If you think I would give all that up to be the impoverished dowager widow of a long-dead boy, you've lost your head.

And I was dazzled by Henry. Not just because of his looks or his energy. He was a golden prince, with a rosebud mouth and hair like a crown. And he was tall, built like a stag. He might have been inferior to Arthur in temperament, but he was enchanting. Always dancing, singing, running, jumping, eating, hunting, jousting. All the energy of youth. And, of course, as far as God and I were concerned, we had been rightfully betrothed for years. Plus, he was my way out of poverty.

We needed the Pope to agree. I had been his brother's wife, and according to the Bible (Leviticus, actually), a man who lies with his brother's wife will not have children with her. But of course, the book of Deuteronomy says a man should marry the childless widow of his brother. So. Bit of a contradiction.

And on a bright June morning, just two months after my father-in-law died, we were married in a small chapel outside Greenwich Palace. I wore a white satin dress with my hair down to really make the virgin point. At twenty-three, the most famous virgin in the world. He was just a boy of eighteen.

I vowed to remain humble and loyal to Henry, and he, Sir Loyal Heart, to me. And because he was young and in awe of me, I thought I could manage him. I thought I could harness his energy, temper his impulsiveness, and make him into a thoughtful ruler, that we might forge ahead as my parents had done.

The coronation, on Midsummer Day, was a bit more of a fancy affair than our wedding. We went through the streets of London together in a blaze of white and gold to show the people what we were about. Wealth, power, style, glamour on display. Even Thomas More said I looked as if I were descended from the great kings.

A few days after our coronation, Henry's old grandmother, Margaret Beaufort, finally let her grip slip on life. And after seven years, I was finally Queen of England.

It is no *arrogancia* to say that I was the perfect Tudor wife. Not only did the very blood in my veins legitimise Henry's rule and guarantee him the power of Spain, with which England could keep pesky France in a vice's grip, but I was also beautiful, and we were in love.

Henry and I actually had a lot in common. It might not have seemed like it—while he was off hunting and jousting, I was busy running the kingdom. But we got along because we shared a devotion to the Church and a passion for the people of England. He saw himself as Defender of the Faith, fascinated by my stories of the campaigns against the unbelieving Moors. He made me recite them as bedtime stories, but he never took the true lessons: courage, devotion to a higher cause. We were both keen autodidacts, me for knowledge and education's value for its own sake and him for how it made him feel. He saw himself as a scholar of religion.

We were new on our thrones and ready to spend money to have a good time. We were always feasting, singing, dancing. Henry loved to dress up, and I humoured him in pretending I didn't recognise him. Ladies, take care when you pretend to laugh at a man's jokes. He might actually believe he's funny.

But when I felt our baby kick in my stomach, a honeymoon baby, our joy was real. In Richmond Palace the next January, I gave birth to our first child: a little princess. She never even opened her eyes. She was dead, and I had failed.

Henry was disgusted with me. I wasn't perfect anymore. And even though I was pregnant again after a few months, he had his first affair. I knew my role. I bit my tongue. I put aside my high-minded intelligence and crusading courage to let a boy humiliate me in public. I never complained. I never told him no. I grew his son inside me while he was tumbling his whore over town. The death of our first baby was a tragedy, but I was about to show him that it had been a one-off: that I was still a good wife and queen.

And I got my reward: on the first day of the year in 1511, our son was born. Henry, we named him. Everything I'd suffered, everything I'd been through and all the years I'd waited, were worth it. And the country went *loco*. Wine flowed from the fountains and fools feasted in the streets. It was a blessing on our marriage and a sign from God that the Tudor reign was approved. Jousts, tourneys, Mass, processions, beacons, we did it all. He was christened, in all the swag we could muster, at Richmond Palace. And two months later, my baby was dead. And I lost something inside me I'd never get back.

Things were never the same between Henry and me, either. There was just too much pain and disappointment. He never forgave me for his dead prince, and I never forgave him for not caring as much as I did.

But we were still rulers, and we still had a job to do. And two years later, when Henry went off to fight in France in 1513, I was left to defend the country from the invasion of the Scots in the North—from James IV, his brother-in-law. Henry might not have loved me as he once did, but he still trusted me, and he leaned on me to keep the country safe. So, Henry made me regent: co-ruler.

When the Scots inevitably invaded—as Scots are wont to do—I was the one taking care of it. And when I met the Scottish king, Henry's sister's husband, on the Flodden Field battlefield, it was my first victory. While Henry played at puny, empty battles in tiny one-horse towns in France, I kept England safe. I led the troops in my armour, and I addressed them as a captain. Once I'd won, I even sent Henry some of the dead Scots king's coat.

Oh, and I did it all while heavily pregnant.

But my father betrayed us. He had persuaded Henry to go to war, to go off on his own crusade against the hated French. It soon became clear that my father was only using Henry and his armies to distract the French. He went off behind our backs and signed a treaty that drew together Spain, France, and the Holy Roman Empire into a great European lion at the feast while England was cast as the bald vulture. The resentment still echoes through your time, I'm sure.

And Henry didn't trust me after that. I was tarnished for him. I was a failure not only as a wife but now as an ally, too. I'm not sure my father ever really understood that. And when I gave birth to another son in September, a tiny premature baby who died soon after, Henry started to believe that I couldn't bear a living child at all.

The next year, the country's coffers were empty after our wars. I gave birth to my third son, my last son, who died almost before he lived. And Henry started to look elsewhere.

The first was Elizabeth "Bessie" Blount, one of my young ladies-in-waiting. No, Anne Boleyn wasn't the first, or even the second. Bessie was, I suppose. She was the official mistress when she was just a teenager. Henry took up with her for *years*.

I knew what I was supposed to do. I'd watched my mother skilfully outmanoeuvre mistress after mistress of my father's by finding their husbands positions far, far away. And he always came back to her. But then again, she'd managed a living son. I'd had another son, by that point, but he was dead in minutes.

I thought Henry's fertile ground of privilege and indulgence could be harnessed by my piety and intelligence, like an

English garden blooming with rain. God help me, I was wrong. Because a leopard cannot change his spots, nor can a spoilt, overindulged, and undisciplined boy ever hope to grow to be a loyal, constant lover. Give a spoilt boy an ax and he becomes a man who chops down trees. Or chops off heads.

After I gave birth to Mary in 1516—at last, a surviving child, my precious *hija*—I thought things would change. I thought I'd overcome whatever issue was killing my babies. My daughter continued to grow even though I checked her breathing like a hawk. But as far as Henry was concerned, a girl was worth *nada*.

DID YOU KNOW?

- I swore that I had never slept with Arthur and that I was a virgin when I married Henry.

- Even Henry's own sister, Mary Tudor (Queen of France), supported my case in the King's Great Matter.

- In my last letter to Henry, in the last months of my life, I called him my "most dear Lord, King, and husband." I was humble and loyal to the end.

And I wasn't young anymore. My prince was just coming into his prime, but I was tired from all the years of poverty and grief. After my last pregnancy in 1518 ended too early, a little girl too young to even have proper lungs to breathe, I was never pregnant again.

That last dead baby changed me forever. I turned to God for strength and began to wear a hair shirt—an undergarment made of coarse, scratchy sackcloth—as penance. I wasn't sexy to Henry anymore. But I never told him no.

And the next year, Bessie gave birth to a bouncing baby boy like a horse drops a foal in a field. Henry even acknowledged the bastard as his own son, calling him Henry Fitzroy. Can you imagine the insult? But I never complained. I never gave *him* cause for complaint.

I never said no to him for anything, not even when he had two children with the Great Whore Mary Boleyn—another of my very own ladies-in-waiting, and this time my own favourite maid.

And then he met her sister. And my husband lost his head and asked me for an annulment. And I said no. No way.

So I didn't let him take the easy way, and we came to blows. Or, as the Americans call it, litigation.

They tried to do it all behind my back, you know, nice and quietly. The King's Great Matter, but they didn't want the public to know. The arrogant *pendejos* didn't even think I'd find out. But they underestimated the loyalty of the people to a twenty-four-year queen. I knew within hours. My marriage on trial, and they didn't even tell me. So I fought back. And he went public, to shame me.

They asked me to enter a convent so the Pope could dissolve the marriage and forget about the original dispensation. A way out for everyone. I could have been gracious. I could have given in. But they didn't know what they were asking of me. They didn't realise that by asking me to join a convent for worldly reasons, they were asking me to turn my back on my true faith. Sacrilege. I had been called to married life, and they asked me to throw that away.

Wolsey, Henry, Campeggio, Clement, all those men could play around with canons and Bible passages and twist their words and desires to suit their desires as much as they liked. But I couldn't. And I wouldn't. A nunnery? *Por favor*.

If Henry had been in his right mind, if it hadn't been turned, he would have understood that he had asked for something I could never give. To deny the marriage was to deny my daughter her rightful place as princess and heir. When he asked me to deny the marriage, he asked me to deny that we should have had dispensation from the Pope. To deny the authority of the Vatican, and the sanctity of the Holy Seal, the integrity of my parents. It wasn't that I chose to say no. It's that there was never a chance I could say yes.

What he never understood, not then or ever after, is that by telling him no I was trying to protect his soul. The ingratitude! Being a wife is a thankless task.

But he still couldn't divorce me. To divorce me, or to put me aside, would have been to admit that our marriage was proper and just. I mean, we were married for twenty-four years. But instead, he had to think highly of himself. He insisted that my marriage to his brother, Arthur, was the one that was real and valid, and that it *had* been consummated, that I had *not* come to his bed a virgin.

They thought I would crumble. They thought I would give in to the agonising blackmail of being separated from my child, my one living child, who was burning up with fever and I couldn't go to her.

But I stuck to my guns because I knew my cause was true. I refused to give in to shame or embarrassment. Trust me, neither get you anywhere. But the lesson here is that something you've fought to your last breath for isn't necessarily worth it. I sacrificed everything for my convictions, which don't pay the rent. I died in cold and discomfort, far from my child.

Here's what I learnt, in nearly a quarter century. Constancy, resilience, tenacity will get you very far. But you will break if you do not bend. There are times to stand firm and times to admit defeat. I did what I had to do, and for that I have no regrets, but no good deed goes unpunished.

The other wives? A few months here, a few years there? I was everything to Henry for half his life. My whole life, I was a pawn in the machinations of lesser men. I was the perfect Tudor wife, and my husband was a feckless whore. I was in the right, my daughter was in the right, we behaved impeccably and had the moral high ground, and still we *lost*. It happens, you know. It's not weak to accept that. *Eso sí que es*, as my mother would have said. It goes how it goes.

I could have gracefully sidestepped like the second "divorcee"–a Flanders mare, you'll meet her later–and I could have salvaged everything. I could have gone home to Spain. But at least I died with my conscience clean, guaranteed of my place in Heaven.

I was born to be Queen of England, and as far as I'm concerned, that's how I died. In the arms of my beloved María, my most loyal friend. Because at the end of it all, your friends are all you have. And that's something that Anne Boleyn would find out, to her cost.

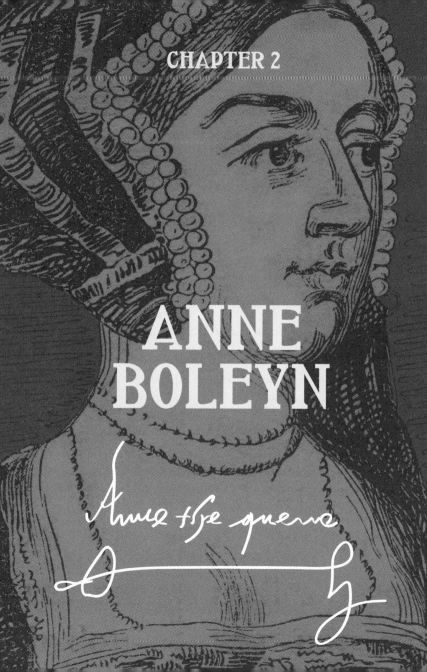

CHAPTER 2

ANNE BOLEYN

PROFILE

NAME: Anne Boleyn (known as Nan), also spelled Anne Bullen, Anna de Boullan, and Anna Bolina

OTHER TITLES: Marquess of Pembroke (1 September 1532 onward)

BORN: May/June 1501 in Norfolk, England

PARENTS: Thomas Boleyn, first Earl of Wiltshire, and Lady Elizabeth Howard

NOTABLE ANCESTORS: Geoffrey Boleyn, Lord Mayor of London in 1457; Thomas Butler, 7th Earl of Ormonde and first Lord Chamberlain to Catherine of Aragon in 1509

SIBLINGS: Mary (born 1499/1500) and George (born approximately 1504)

CHILDHOOD: Grew up in Hever Castle in Kent, was sent to Archduchess Margaret of Austria in Mechelen, Burgundian Netherlands (now Belgium), and then to Queen Claude of France

LOOKS: Dark hair, dark eyes, strong nose, olive skin, slim figure

PERSONALITY: Intelligent, fiery, witty, tempestuous

EDUCATION: Could read and write in Latin, French, and English; was schooled in arithmetic, history, and religion; loved music, card games, and horseback riding

RELIGION: French humanist and Renaissance Christian; supporter of reform and vernacular Bible

MARRIAGES:

- Henry Percy, 5th Earl of Northumberland (betrothed): 1523, age about twenty-two; betrothal was rejected in 1524 by Henry Percy's father and Cardinal Wolsey
- Henry VIII on 25 January 1533, after a secret ceremony in November 1533, age about thirty-one

AGE DIFFERENCE WITH HENRY: About ten years

MOTTO: "The most happy"

CROWNED: 1 June 1533 in Westminster Abbey

CHILDREN: One surviving, two miscarriages, possibly more

- 7 September 1533, a girl, Princess Elizabeth (later Queen Elizabeth I)
- Summer 1534, a stillbirth or miscarriage
- January 1536, a miscarriage (possibly a boy)

MARRIAGE ENDED: 14 May 1536, after three years, when it was declared void by Thomas Cranmer

DIED: 19 May 1536 at the Tower of London, beheaded with a French sword

BURIED: Chapel Royal of St Peter ad Vincula, parish church of the Tower of London (unmarked grave until 1876)

DID YOU KNOW?

❁ I was the last of Henry's wives to be crowned, which makes me his only real queen.

❁ I was crowned with Saint Edward's Crown, which previously had been used only for monarchs.

❁ I was also the first English queen to be publicly executed. My husband hired a French swordsman especially for me because he thought it unseemly to behead his wife with an ax.

❁ When Henry and I learned that Catherine had died in 1536, we wore yellow—the Spanish colour of mourning, the English colour of joy. A subtle insult.

❁ On the day Catherine was buried, I miscarried the baby boy that might have saved my marriage.

❁ There are no existing portraits of me from when I was alive.

❁ My personal emblem was a falcon: a hunting bird of prey.

❁ When I was tried for treason, the jury included my former fiancé, Henry Percy, and my own uncle.

DON'T LOSE YOUR HEAD

Mon Dieu, but she does go on. Couldn't get rid of her in her lifetime, her death was the beginning of the end for mine, and still she's whining. All I can say to her is, you think you had it bad? Try having your neck chopped.

Whore, they called me. The concubine. The witch. The monster who cursed the Tudors. With six fingers on one hand and a deformed lump on my neck. Why are you so obsessed with me, all these centuries later? Just like my husband. Henry lost his head over me. It's ironic that I lost mine over him.

As a matter of fact, I was the last of Henry's wives to actually be crowned. Because his marriage to Catherine was declared null and void, that makes me his only real queen. I died, but I deserved to win.

 CATHERINE: *Er, hang on. You spent seven years trying to take him from me—and you lost him almost immediately to Jane!*

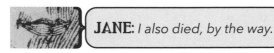 **JANE:** *I also died, by the way.*

Shut up, Jane. You're still the one that everybody loves.

I was never a whore. I was just *hot*. But I kept it on a pedestal.
I wasn't so easy as my sister Mary, or so unfussy as Henry's
big mistress, Bessie Blount. How could anyone call me a
whore when my very success depended on my *not* giving
him what he wanted? In fact, I refused to sleep with him.
Seven long years I kept that dog on the scent, without ever
once letting him chow down.

The truth is, it wasn't my fault that Henry got his marriage
annulled. I might have given him a fixation, but he was
already trying to get rid of her. The pressure was on for him
to have a son, and he was saddled with an old wife who
had given him nothing but dead babies. And I wasn't even
the first Boleyn to know it. We'll get to that.

I might have been a commoner, but my grandfather the
Earl of Surrey was one of the top dogs in England. My
mother was Lady Elizabeth Howard—of the Howard family,
the most prominent in England, *comme vous le savez,* but
she married for love like a fool, and I ended up with Thomas
Boleyn, 1st Earl of Wiltshire, as my father. A commoner but
a clever one, with a gift for languages and the advancement
of his family. Actually, my father was made a Knight of the
Bath in the great coronation of Henry and Catherine.

They did their duty as courtly parents and hoofed me
straight over the sea. First to the Low Countries, where my
father had been an ambassador. Margaret, Archduchess
of Austria and daughter of the Holy Roman Emperor

Maximilian I, ruled the Netherlands on behalf of her nephew Charles. That awkward boy would go on to be Holy Roman Emperor Charles V. After Isabella's death almost a decade before, Margaret of Austria was the most powerful woman in Europe.

In fact, she had been married to Isabella's son Juan—the brother of Catherine of Aragon, Queen of England. So basically, I served Catherine's sister-in-law. She taught me a few things. She refused to remarry after the deaths of her first two husbands and had earned her right to rule alone.

My father's talents impressed her so much that she offered me a place in her household as a courtesy. So there I was, just a girl of twelve, in the household of one of Europe's most impressive women. She babied me, called me La Petite Boulin, and I was happy there. Other children from other noble families were there, too, and it was a place of intellectual and artistic pursuits. Margaret brought all the best from France and Spain to Burgundy, her music, her dance, her art. I was a precocious child and grew up speaking fluent French.

But then they sent me to wait on Henry VIII's sister, Mary, the French Queen, when she went to Paris to marry Louis XII. Then I served her stepdaughter, Queen Claude. I was all but French. And that's where I learned the skills I needed. Of course, I could play cards, dance, hunt, ride, write poetry, and speak three languages. But more than anything, I learned how to beguile.

You see, I wasn't beautiful. I'm not remembered as the most attractive woman in history because of a perfect nose or golden hair. If you ever learn anything from me, learn this: you do not have to look good to be hot. I had beautiful dark eyes, but I was no Hans Holbein painting. I knew how to move, I knew how to capture a man's attention with my wit and passion. Men got hot for my brain more than for my body; they just didn't know it. And if anything proves it, it's the fact that Henry was wild for me for seven years without ever once doing the deed. That's not to say, of course, that I did nothing.

They brought me back to England when I was about twenty to marry my Irish cousin James Butler, 9th Earl of Ormond. Ireland, a land of savages hardly better than Wales! But plans broke off, so where does a young woman go to show off? London, to court. So I was sent to wait on the old Spanish Queen. I, a French courtier, champion of reform, was sent to wait on an old Spanish Catholic who couldn't hang on to her man. Bound to end badly, *n'est-ce pas*?

And I went from being one English paste stone in a French crown to the French jewel in England. The attention kind of went to my head.

I met a man named Henry. No, not Henry VIII. Henry Percy, a young man in the retinue of one Thomas Wolsey, the cardinal who was in charge of the court back then—and of the king. Henry Percy fell for me, hook, line and sinker. The heir to Northumberland, the future earl. One of the most eligible bachelors at court. We had a mad spring fling and secretly became betrothed.

But the truth is that I was only a little bit calculating. Yes, he was powerful; yes, he was wealthy; but I did really love him. And when it all fell apart, it broke whatever compassion and weakness there was left in me.

Because he might have been a catch, but he wasn't so eligible after all. He was betrothed to Mary Talbot, who he didn't even like. But when Cardinal Wolsey and his father found out about our engagement, they refused to let it stand. Wolsey called me a foolish girl, an upstart, and my family sent me back to the family home, Hever Castle. Like a naughty schoolgirl.

My poor Henry was punished and married off to his childhood fiancée, who bitterly despised him because of his love for me. He always resented her because she wasn't me. Both our hearts broke, and it would go on to cause a world of trouble for all of us.

Because I never, ever forgot. I never forgave Wolsey. He took my true love from me, and worse, he shamed me. Bide your time and wait for your revenge. Let no man ever forget that he underestimated you.

So I bided my time. I came back to court stronger, tougher than ever. I dazzled the courtiers, and I became a favourite. But although I might have been the most captivating Boleyn girl, there was another. My elder sister, Mary, wife of William Carey, was the king's mistress.

In fact, most people believe he'd sired her two children—a son, Henry Carey, and a daughter, Catherine—although he never acknowledged them as royal bastards the way he did with Henry Fitzroy. That should have been a big warning flag for me. The king used her, dishonoured her, cuckolded her husband, and ignored their children. *Pas bien*.

I learnt the wrong lesson from my sister. I learnt to hold him off, not to give in. I should have run. Because his spit was barely dry on her mouth before his greedy eyes turned to me.

Oh, did you think it was a calculated seven-year seduction? Yeah, you and everyone else. But even I couldn't have envisaged the stakes of the game I was playing.

 CATHERINE: *What nonsense, Anne. You knew exactly what you were doing.*

Maybe I did, maybe I didn't. But you'll never know for sure. The truth is, I didn't want to be just another mistress, used and cast aside like my sister. I didn't want it all to crumble, like it had with Henry Percy.

And honestly, I respected Queen Catherine—although I'd never have admitted it. She had a brain between her ears, no doubt. But she didn't respect me. She, the Spanish moral compass; I, the silly French tart. She didn't see me as a threat. She was too busy looking at Mary, at Bessie, at the obvious mistresses who gave Henry whatever they wanted. But she should have been looking to her own affairs. Henry knew he could make a son. He'd done it with my sister. He'd done it with Bessie.

It wasn't nearly as much about me as you might think. The truth is, Henry was getting anxious. The queen gave him stillbirth after stillbirth, one puny little girl, and he needed an heir. Catherine must have known that her days were numbered. In fact, he'd spoken to doctors in 1524 about her courses drying up. He was already thinking of getting rid of her—long before he and I were ever involved. His courtiers wanted a new wife for Henry, too. A princess from Portugal, or France, or somewhere useful. But why not me?

This time, I was determined to win. After all, I was the best. Why shouldn't I capture the greatest prize? My sister had the looks, the golden hair, the bountiful womb, the bouncy breasts. She had it all. And two children. And he'd deserted her in the end. And what did I have? My mind. Use what God gave you. I might not have been the schemer everybody thinks, but I wasn't an idiot, either.

As they say, timing is everything. His fervent desire to be rid of his old wife and his equally fervent desire for me managed to coincide. And by 1526, he was *obsessed*. *Mon Dieu*, he wrote me constant letters—unusual for a lazy man who hated writing. I ignored him. I tried to turn him down without actually *turning him down*. Tried to let it gently fizzle out. But he just got more intense. He pushed and pushed and pushed. He didn't take no for an answer.

What was I supposed to say? I had to fall back on my "chastity." It's not as if I could get married while everyone knew he was mad for me.

He wasn't having sex with Catherine anymore, so there was no way he'd get a son there. He needed to be rid of her. And there was only one way out for me: to replace her. But Henry being Henry, he needed to think well of himself. He needed to appear just. It all came down to ego, in the end.

So I showed him how to do it—how he could be rid of a queen. I told him that the old Pope had no right to grant the dispensation, to overrule the Bible. Logically, therefore, the new Pope had to annul the marriage. I told Henry that he should ask the Pope to investigate the marriage because the dispensation had been given under a false pretense: that her marriage to Arthur had been consummated. That Henry's marriage to Catherine was cursed.

And that's what he did. We broke cover, and suddenly the whole of Europe knew what I was about.

It should have been *so* easy. Jesus, it could have been done in weeks. The Pope had already granted annulments to other kings. But it all went to *merde*, and we ended up in seven years of legal machinations.

It didn't really help that at one point the Pope was the prisoner of Charles V, the Holy Roman Emperor and loyal nephew of Catherine of Aragon. It turns out, putting aside a daughter of Spain is quite the big deal.

And Wolsey thought he was doing it all for a French princess. He preferred the French to the Spanish, and he thought they'd be easier to control. But this silly little girl was French at heart. And while he was off on the King's Great Matter in Europe, I supplanted him. He came back to find that I was in charge. And I got my revenge.

In fairness, I thought Catherine would go. I thought she would *want* the easy way out. I projected my own selfishness onto her. I didn't know what she'd endured to get to where she was. I saw only what I saw on the throne, and I didn't see what she had done to get there.

But then came the Sweat. A pandemic that stopped everything. And Henry found that his sexual obsession for me was no match for his fear of illness and rank disease. He fled like a baby to a wife who was more mother, fell back on his habit and the comfort of the familiar, and ran like a little bitch. He didn't even visit—he sent his doctor to me. I was humanised for him, and not in a good way. Best never let a man see you sweat.

It killed my maids. It killed my poor brother-in-law, William Carey. My sister was almost broke, and I had to beg Henry for an allowance for her. He gave it but moaned about her loose ways. Which is somewhat ironic.

Meanwhile, Henry and Catherine moved like blessed lambs from palace to palace without ever even perspiring. So I had to reconcile with Wolsey or, at least, pretend to. I have to tell you, there's nothing like a near-death experience in a pandemic to knock the stuffing out of you.

But when I returned to court in London in the winter, I had my own suite of apartments. There were two queens at court. God, by this point, I *had* to see it through to the end. How the hell was I ever going to make another good marriage again?

And so we went to trial. Queen Catherine was called to court. And she refused to go! She said she wouldn't accept an English trial and referred our case to a higher court: God. In Rome, that is to say. She shamed him, before all the people, his sham court, and his sham judges. She asked how she could possibly have offended him. She swore that Arthur had never had her. Who knows, maybe she was telling the truth. Although it didn't matter anyway.

She said that she had been a true, humble, and obedient wife. She pointed out that God had not cursed their marriage with childlessness—that, in fact, they had had many children, whom God had called out of the world.

In fairness, it was magnificent. It almost made me want to cheer. If she hadn't been thwarting everything in my path, I probably would have done so. Because she was totally right. She never did a thing wrong as a wife, apart from failing to provide a son, and I would come to learn that that wasn't her fault, either. She stood up for every legitimate wife, every good woman, and every true soul—none of which I was.

But she put it to his conscience, and she walked out! Never underestimate the power of a well-timed exit. Sometimes a bit of drama is called for. She never came back.

The trial dragged on all summer long. Apparently, Arthur said he "had been in Spain" all night. Always be wary of a man who brags about his conquests. If a man swears he has had a woman and a woman swears he did no such thing, who are you going to believe, really?

And Henry had to keep me out of sight, to keep pretending that he wanted rid of Catherine because of his good conscience and not because of his hard cock.

Henry was *furious*. He needed someone to blame for all these delays, for making him wait all those years to have me, even as I got older and became less of a fantasy, more of a drama. I had to engineer petty screaming fights and steamy make-ups just to keep him interested.

He couldn't blame Catherine. She was way too popular. So he decided to blame Wolsey. I had absolutely nothing to do with that decision. Nothing whatsoever. Definitely just a coincidence. Henry stripped Wolsey of the chancellorship and arrested him. But the wily old man managed to die on me. I still got his palace, though.

And bit by bit, I kept taking over. When the Archbishop of Canterbury died the following year, I managed to get our Boleyn family chaplain appointed: Thomas Cranmer.

And in 1523, an ambitious young lawyer called Thomas Cromwell came up and, over the years, passed some laws to make it official: that England now had supremacy over its own church. That we had broken with Rome. And Henry's beloved Thomas More resigned.

Even before Henry and I were married, diplomats had to kowtow to me. I was at his side in matters of state long before I was in his bed for matters of sex. Power is what you make it. Henry made me Marquess of Pembroke, the most powerful woman in the country. You don't need a ring to make a stir. So when we went to Calais together in the winter of 1532 to get some support from Francis I for our marriage, that's exactly what I did. I made a stir.

But Francis couldn't explicitly go against the Pope. So when we came back to Dover, we just did it. It was a quick, anticlimactic end to a long-drawn-out drama. We were quietly married in secret, in November 1532. And I'd done it, at last. Seven long years. Nobody thought it could be done.

Things moved quickly. Cranmer convened the court to rule on the marriage to Catherine of Aragon and declared it void. Five days later, he declared ours valid. The Commons forbade any appeals to Rome, so Catherine had no recourse. And they sent her into exile, and I was crowned Queen of England in my own right. And Henry was Supreme Head of the Church of England.

My motto was "The most happy." I suppose I was, when I quickly got pregnant. Henry thought that God was smiling on him.

And then I had a girl. He wasn't best pleased. All that work, for Henry to get another girl. How they must have laughed. When my daughter was born, we had to quickly add a couple of s's on the end of letters that all announced the birth of a prince. Never count your chickens, and so forth.

Princess Mary, now the bastard Lady Mary, was sent to Hatfield House to help care for the baby. I named her Elizabeth.

And everything began to fall apart. Henry and I started to fight. Because what a man loves in a mistress and idealises in a lover, he rarely likes in a wife. And I'd already disappointed him. We spent and spent to persuade people to get on board with our new court. Feasts and jousting and renovated palaces. We spent money to buy people's approval. Surprise, surprise, it didn't work. People *hated* me for it. They blamed me for Henry's growing abuse of his own power and called me a whore. And he blamed me for the loss of their love.

And when I had my first miscarriage in 1534, Henry hated me, too. By the following October, I was pregnant again. I was…what, thirty-five? Thirty-six? It was maybe my last chance.

Then came 1536, the year everything changed. First, Catherine of Aragon died. She had never given in; she had never let go. The spectre at the feast of my marriage was dead.

And yeah, I celebrated. I danced on her grave. I wore yellow, the colour of mourning in Spain but a joyful colour in the Tudor court, because only the smartest of the courtiers could understand the subtle insult. Of course, the Spanish ambassador was furious. But I didn't do it because I was the "most happy." Not really.

And then there were rumours, whispers that Henry and I had poisoned her. As if I needed to! She was *ancient* by then, at least fifty, and she looked every minute of it. Plus, you know, the hair shirt. But when they cut her corpse open, they found some black lump on her heart. As if she had died of her grief.

And Henry wasn't even that sad. I mean, he acted as though he was. After all, he'd loved her for at least fifteen years. She'd almost killed herself trying to give him sons. I'm not totally heartless. I was there; I saw how much she suffered.

But the truth is, when Henry turned away from a woman, he rarely looked back. He didn't even say goodbye. Not to her, and not to me. In his mind, she'd trapped him in a princeless sham marriage and defied him when he tried to be rid of her. She was already dead to him.

What he felt, actually, was guilt. He knew he'd done her wrong; he knew she'd died a blameless woman in cold, damp heartbreak. Deep down, he knew. But a man like Henry can't bear to feel guilty, and so he looks to put the blame elsewhere to feel better. In this case, on me.

Anyway, I don't need to tell you that he never poisoned Catherine. If Henry and I had really wanted to kill her, we could have done it in public, with a whole lot of pomp. We even kept her funeral procession out of sight, buried in the backwaters near Peterborough. That said, the common people did flock to the coffin of "Queen Catherine."

They understood what I didn't. I might have celebrated her death, but I didn't realise how vulnerable it made me. I thought her cause in the King's Great Matter had died with her. But think about it: all those people who thought that her marriage was still valid and that therefore I was some kind of glorified mistress? As far as they were concerned, Henry was now single again. And I was the whore who had bewitched him away from his true wife. He could wake up from the spell.

And that's where Jane Seymour entered the ring.

 JANE: *That's not quite fair, is it, Anne? It's not like it was much of a competition by then.*

Jane, *mon Dieu*, I'm still talking. You stole my husband from me while I was rotting in the Tower. You're not stealing my moment in the spotlight here.

Ah, but you know, she's not wrong. I might have been pregnant, but Henry was barely talking to me.

Henry was starting to suspect that our marriage would never be taken seriously—not on the continent or in the English hills. People kept hinting that it would be to Henry's advantage if he were considering another wife.

The court was full of my enemies, and the Seymour vultures were circling. She even had a brand-new bed. Ladies, take note. If your man is paying more attention to the throw pillows of your maid than your own, that's a problem. I once walked into a room to find Jane, the so-called saint, wriggling in his lap.

And then, in a jousting tournament, something unthinkable happened that none of us could have seen coming. The king was knocked off his horse, which opened an old wound on his leg that had never really healed. We thought he was going to die. And who would've been his heir? The bastard Lady Mary? My tiny princess? How was it going to work? The court was in disarray.

Between the death of Catherine and the near death of my husband, and his carrying on with Jane, the stress of it all got to me. And I miscarried my last baby, on the day of Catherine's funeral. That was the beginning of the end.

That was my son. Yeah, Catherine and I had royal princes, too, you know, Jane. Just because they didn't survive—through no fault of our own—doesn't mean they didn't count, that they weren't perfect. I didn't understand that before I had my own child. I genuinely didn't care when Catherine miscarried.

 CATHERINE: *Jesus, Anne, not even woman to woman?*

Nope. Really didn't. All your dead little babies let me teach Henry that your marriage was cursed. That he'd never have a live son off you. They disgusted him. And I fanned that. But I never realised, until I had my own child, that every miscarriage or stillbirth is a baby you didn't have. I wish I'd known that when you were alive.

 CATHERINE: *I wish you had, too.*

So Henry used my miscarriage, our poor dead son, as a way to accuse me of all sorts of things. Of seducing him into the marriage. Of treason. Of adultery. Of all the ugliest things.

I tried everything. I tried bridging the divide with my uncle. I even tried mending fences with Cromwell. But they weren't exactly well disposed to me.

And in April, my brother George, 2nd Viscount Rochford, didn't get the Order of the Garter, which was some bigshot male prize. My uncle refused to help me. I had no friends left, no loyal courtiers or powerful allies. I'd alienated everyone in my rise to the top. So when I began to slip, nobody saw fit to lend a hand.

I didn't know it then, but Henry signed something— at Cromwell's behest, I imagine—to appoint the Lord Chancellor and some other nobles to investigate something—or someone.

Mark Smeaton, my poor little lute player, was arrested. I swear, I never did anything with him. *Mon Dieu*, he was practically a boy! How could I, who had won over the greatest man in the world, possibly have had my head turned by a silly strumming child.

But even queens get lonely. And I'll admit it, I did play around with his emotions a bit. But they racked the poor boy; they tortured him like the commoner he was. They racked him like an animal, pulled him apart 'til the only thing twanging were his ribs. And, of course, he confessed. I'm not sure what to—I doubt, in his agony, even he knew—but it was enough to sink us all.

May Day, May Day. *M'aidez*. The first day of May, or my last day of freedom. At the tournament, I was still seated beside Henry as his wife and queen, but I knew it was only a matter of time. It was hot, unseasonably hot, and I was sweating like a common pig. I should have trusted my gut; I should have made my excuses and left. But I was too proud, too scared, too utterly *fucked* by my own flirtation with danger. I couldn't have moved even if I wanted to.

Henry got some message, a note from his page, and he heaved himself out of his chair, beckoning Henry Norris to come with him. That was the last I saw of him. He'd torn the world apart for me, but when he left me he never looked back. He didn't say goodbye. That was the moment I knew it was all over for me.

ANNE BOLEYN

Henry took Henry Norris to the Tower. God knows what Mark Smeaton had said about him. Two days later, my friend Sir Francis Weston was arrested, and Sir William Brereton, my privy chamber groom. Then Thomas Wyatt, my old friend. All the young men who had drunk together, ridden together, written poetry together, gambled, feasted, danced, played music.

And on the second day in May, it was my turn to face the music. I should have been flattered, really, that a great rise like mine would warrant a great fall. I was accused of adultery. I was accused of incest with my brother. I was accused of high treason: of plotting to murder the king. But the worst part? One of the men who read me the charges was my uncle. And Henry was nowhere to be seen.

DID YOU KNOW?

People remember that I was accused of being a witch, but the official indictments never said so.

They also say I had six fingers on my right hand. I definitely did not.

I'm remembered for my selfishness, but I actually argued that some of the Church's wealth should be given to charity. Cromwell disagreed; it went straight into the king's wallet.

They literally sent me down the river, from Greenwich Palace to the Tower of London. The last time I'd been there, it was for my coronation. They even let me have my old room. In my very last letter to Henry, I told him that I didn't know why I had been imprisoned. I told him that I was the most loyal wife—well-chosen words, considering that fool still called himself Sir Loyal Heart.

Truth be told, I went a bit ballistic. I couldn't stop crying and raging—perhaps it was still the hormones from my miscarriage—although I'd never had much of a handle on my temper. But in fairness, I was being accused of adultery. What's the penalty for cheating on the king? Oh, only getting seared at the stake like so much *filet mignonne*.

Plus, my trial was a total sham.

 **CATHERINE:** *How ironic.*

Isn't it, just? But it was nothing like yours, Catherine. I had no great allies in Rome or much popularity with the people. They didn't even try to make it look like a real inquiry. That trial had one purpose, and one purpose only: to get rid of me. Nobody *really* thought I'd been with my brother, for God's sake. They might have doubted my chastity, they might have suspected my virtue, but they didn't really think I'd slept with all those men while pregnant with the king's child, either. But Henry had decided I had to go.

I begged him for a lawful trial; I pleaded with him not to let my enemies be my judges. It was, after all, rather unfortunate that I'd made an enemy of so many men.

I was confused, angry, betrayed, terrified. I was all the things that I'd made Catherine feel, and suddenly, I was sorry for it.

 **CATHERINE:** *Too little, too late.*

I wasn't nearly so callous as you might think—I didn't beg only for my life. I begged for the life of my brother and the lives of all the other innocent men he'd arrested. Weston, Brereton, Norris, even little Smeaton, who by then was so demented from the pain of torture that he'd pleaded guilty. And by the time it came to my trial, on 15 May, all of them had already been sentenced to death.

So there we were, my brother George and I, in the Great Hall of the Tower of London, a spectacle for the two thousand people in the stands. And there was our uncle, the Duke of Norfolk, presiding over us like a spectre of our past glory.

But what was worse, *far* worse, was that in the sea of faces that stood to judge me, was my old love, Henry Percy. By then, he'd become Earl of Northumberland, but the years of bitter disappointment with his wife Mary Talbot and his heartbreak over losing me had withered him. Honestly, I barely recognised him at first. But when I finally cottoned on, I thought I was going to vomit. Imagine, after all those years, in my darkest moment, him still having that effect on me. I guess it's true what they say: you never really get over your first loves.

And he certainly didn't get over me. When the verdict came back, he collapsed.

I did much better. I stayed calm, collected, convincing. Much good it did me. They found me guilty anyway.

And what kills me (well, what killed me) was that they used my own words to do it. They brought George's vile wife, Lady Rochford—or Jane Parker, as I used to know her before she married my brother—into his trial to speak against him. She claimed that we were overfamiliar, *incestuous*, just because he preferred my company to hers. And frankly, who wouldn't?

I mean, did you ever *meet* Jane Parker? Although I suppose you didn't have to—what kind of woman sends her husband to such a death? You see, he was accused of high treason, too, as well as incest and adultery with me. My poor George might have escaped the sentence of hanged, drawn, and quartered, but that was just a small mercy from the king.

So guess what Lady Rochford told the court? *She* said that *I'd* said that Henry couldn't make love to his wife. That he couldn't get it up.

Good God, but the ego of him! He was getting old, my dear husband, and his leg was completely wrecked from his fall. He certainly wasn't much good in the sack after that. So no, I never said it, but yeah, it was still true. Word to the wise. Men don't take kindly to having their sexual shortcomings play out in open court. For Christ's sake, she *read it out*.

My sister-in-law, my lady-in-waiting, my former colleague. She damned me with those words; she damned my brother, her own husband and the father of her son. She damned us all, and she damned herself. *Why?*

All these years, and I still haven't figured it out. Was she really so petty and vindictive as to bring down the whole family out of jealousy? Because I was beautiful and George loved me?

I guess we'll never know. And I guess it doesn't matter. Because with those words I was done, and George was done, and it was done. And all there was left for us to do was beg for a merciful way to die.

He ordered an executioner from France: a Calais swordsman in preference of a blunt English ax. I must say, it did seem slightly more elegant. A fancy French sword for a fancy French neck. You have to laugh, right?

So that's how I ended up watching from the window of my cell in the Tower as my friends and brother were executed. I saw George's lips move as he gave his last speech to the crowd, who were just there for a fun day out. I don't know what he said, but he stood straight. As I pressed my hands against the glass, I prayed to have the same strength.

Unfortunately, I had to wait a bit longer. You see, my beloved husband—who by that point was already snuggled up with Seymour—had to make a last grand gesture. He had to have Archbishop Cranmer declare our marriage invalid. Why? God knows. Our own family chaplain, no less! Cranmer was my invention, and he turned on me.

What a waste of time. And problematic, too. If our marriage was invalid, how could I have committed adultery? Perhaps he did it just to make my baby Elizabeth a bastard, like Mary, to leave the line of succession wide open in case he managed to get any calves off of Jane.

The decree that declared our marriage invalid in May actually went through in June, *after* he was already married to Jane Seymour. Kind of overkill, seeing as I was already dead.

And when my day finally came, I forgave Henry. I called him a gentle, merciful prince and a good, gentle lord. Tongue firmly in my cheek, teeth gritted, but I still did it, if only for the sake of my daughter. I gave a full confession to the archbishop and received the full sacrament—but I admitted nothing. No guilt.

CATHERINE: *That's what convinced me that she was innocent. I still think she would've confessed in that moment, when it didn't matter either way, if there had been something to confess.*

JANE: *I don't know. Don't you think she did that for Elizabeth, too?*

CATHERINE: *Hard to say. Anne might have been self-serving, but she was never a fool.*

Girls, I'm still talking. Anyway. If you learn anything from me, learn this. If you have to die, die with your head up and your chest out—if only so the sword of Calais gets good purchase.

So I walked to that green with my head held up. The dread of the thing is always worse than the thing itself, and so it was with my own execution. I wore a red petticoat and a fur-trimmed gown—after all, just because you're going to die doesn't mean you shouldn't look your best. A little bit of leg goes a long way, especially when you've got no head.

Mine is still one of the most famous faces in the world. I turned Henry's head, and he never turned back. I made history: Beat that, Jane. But take note. Be careful what you wish for. And if you dance on another woman's grave, for sure there will be one who dances on yours. Karma was a bigger bitch than she was. But I guess I should let her tell it.

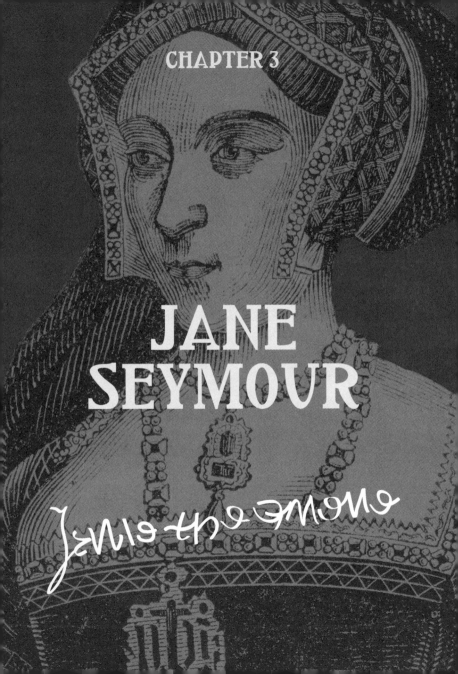

CHAPTER 3

JANE SEYMOUR

PROFILE

NAME: Jane Seymour

BORN: 1509 (?)

PARENTS: Sir John Seymour of Wolf Hall and Margery Wentworth

NOTABLE ANCESTORS: Lionel of Antwerp, 1st Duke of Clarence

SIBLINGS: John (born ?), Edward (born 1500?), Henry (born 1503), Thomas (born 1508?), John, Anthony, Margery (born ?), Dorothy (born 1515?), Elizabeth (born 1518?)

CHILDHOOD: Born in Wolf Hall, Wiltshire, grew up in the country life, later served Catherine of Aragon at court and became maid of honour in 1532

EDUCATION: Not formally educated but had basic literacy; skilled in embroidery, needlework, and household management

LOOKS: Pale, medium height, fair-haired, placid face

PERSONALITY: Gentle, polite, kind, meek, conservative, formal

RELIGION: Roman Catholic, a member of the Third Order of Saint Francis (would later be portrayed as a Protestant)

Married Henry: 30 May 1536 at the Palace of Whitehall, age approximately twenty-eight; proclaimed queen 4 June but never crowned

Age difference: Approximately sixteen years

MOTTO: "Bound to obey and serve"

CHILDREN: One surviving, one miscarriage

- Christmas 1536, miscarriage
- 12 October 1537, a boy, Edward VI (later King Edward VI)

MARRIAGE ENDED: In 1537, after a year, on her death

DIED: 24 October 1537, of complications after birth or possibly an infection, age about twenty-nine

BURIED: Saint George's Chapel, Windsor Castle

DID YOU KNOW?

- Through my grandfather, I was related to King Edward III's son, Lionel of Antwerp. That made Henry my fifth cousin.

- My great-grandmother, Elizabeth Cheney, was also the great-grandmother of Anne Boleyn and Katherine Howard.

- When the king was hitting on me but still married to Anne, I returned his gifts to show off my virtue.

- He did give me a locket with his portrait, which Anne ripped off my neck.

- Henry proposed to me the day he beheaded Anne. We were married ten days later.

- I was never crowned as queen. Henry said it was because of the plague in London, but I suspected he was waiting for me to prove myself with a son.

- My biggest pregnancy craving was for quail, which Henry sourced from continental Europe.

- My personal emblem was a phoenix rising from a burning castle.

- I was the only one of the six to receive a queen's funeral.

JANE SEYMOUR

For the record, I never danced on her grave. I might not have been her biggest fan, but I prayed for her when she died.

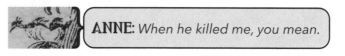

ANNE: *When he killed me, you mean.*

Either way. I prayed for you. You didn't deserve to die. But I wasn't sorry you were gone.

Whatever you think you know about me, you're wrong. They remember me as a saint, the only woman Henry loved, after the end of his cursed first marriage and the execution of his wicked second. They remember me as the generic Jane with a dull face and a guileless mind. An immovable prude with a heart of stone. The perfect antidote to Anne Boleyn's poison.

But the truth is, you don't really know me. You think I didn't act exactly as Anne did? She took seven years to do it. I was on Henry's lap within months. Look, I'm still modest, but you take your wins where you can. I wasn't a saint by any means. I wasn't a dull foil for Anne. He wasn't with me because I was the antidote. He was with me because I was always the perfect wife for him.

I might not have been a saint, but I was plain and honest, and here's the plain and honest truth: I loved him. Tormented as he was by Anne's wild ways, he was happy to follow me back into the light of true faith and into the bed of a good woman. I knew I could be the wife he needed. Like my motto said, I was bound to obey and serve. And that's what I did.

Really, there were only two proper wives: Catherine of Aragon and me. She was his true queen until she died, bless her, and I was the one who gave him the son he needed. His true love. The other four don't count—*especially* Anne.

But after Queen Catherine, with her high-minded moral purpose, he needed someone like me in his later years. Someone who wouldn't try to rule alongside him or challenge him but would appease him and comfort him. I knew my place, and that was by his side, slightly behind. That was where I stood. Until, of course, I died drowning in my own fever sweat, crying for my husband who wasn't there.

And so, I was the only one of all the six to get a queen's funeral. The only one to die in favour and triumph. Even after I was dead, Henry looked for me in the faces of all the women who came along. He still used my face for every painting. And when it was his turn to die, in great pain and misery, he was buried beside me on his request. And so, in that way, I outlived all the other wives. Unlike Catherine

Parr, the last one, who ended up marrying my brother right after Henry's death. She'll tell you all about that, I'm sure.

Look, I know that I didn't have as much to put up with as the later wives. Not the disregard for Anna of Cleves nor the cruelty to little Katherine Howard. Yes, I saw that, and I wasn't impressed. But the only reason that Henry went the way he did was that he was devastated by my death.

And I know I didn't have as much or as long with him as the first two. But bear in mind, I also married a different Henry. Catherine got the prince she moulded into a king; Anne tormented him into a powerful majesty without peer in Europe. The golden prince and the tawny lion. And what did I get? I got the grumpy tyrant, furious at Anne and himself. Already fat, balding, middle-aged, stubby-fingered, and possibly impotent. And I loved him anyway.

But the sad truth is, Henry truly loved me only after I was dead. All that saintly stuff? Posthumous suck-up. Sheer, self-serving baloney. I might have loved him, but I'm not so stupid as you thought. Judge a man on how he treats his wife in life, not how he remembers her in death.

And here's another truth: I killed him. It was my death that sent him down the path of tyranny, of greed, of insatiable lust and horrible cruelty. After my death, Henry began to bloat with grief, and he never really stopped.

My childhood was not nearly as glamorous as Queen Catherine's nor so foreign and exotic as Anne's or Anna's. And I was not so educated as Queen Catherine, but I was related to her. The Seymours were still an ancient and important family. My mother, Margery Wentworth, had that little bit of royalty that was so intoxicating to the Tudor court. Through her mother, I was descended from King Edward III. I even shared a grandmother with Catherine—and with Anne Boleyn, too, although the Seymours prefer to forget that. They also prefer to forget that my father, Sir John Seymour, was there at the Field of the Cloth of Gold with Anne's father, Thomas, and Henry in 1520.

I was born in Wolf Hall, Wiltshire, which is where my romance with Henry would later begin. It was the family seat of the Seymours, but it was hardly a palace. Actually, it was a quiet country life of garden herbs and fireside sewing. I was one of ten, so nothing special, but the eldest girl and a healthy child from clearly fertile stock. I'm not even sure of the year. I grew up with no formal education or spark of excitement. I could read and write a little in English, but I wasn't stupid. People think of me as bovine, docile, but I poured my frustrated hopes and vivacity into my embroidery.

A pale, symmetrical child, not one destined for high jinks, perhaps, but a sturdy choice. Like a good palfrey. There's a lot to be said for that. And because nobody saw me as a threat, I stole a prize from under everyone's noses. You see, my parents were eager for me to marry William Dormer, son of Sir Robert Dormer. But Lady Dormer thought me too low for her son. I admit it: I was disappointed. But I went on to the greatest place in the kingdom. I imagine that had her sucking on her teeth.

I was no great beauty, but I was good-natured and even-tempered, and sometimes that's all you need to be. It's okay to not be a showstopper. And unlike Anne, I never showed my sexual side, so men never feared me.

I joined the court relatively late, when I was about twenty. Since I hadn't grown up there, I wasn't well versed in two-faced flirtation. I had to learn, and learn fast, how to survive in what was becoming the most dangerous court in the world.

At that time, things were moving faster in the city than any of us stuck in the plodding countryside had realised. Our beloved King Henry had decided to throw off his wife, asking the Pope for an annulment and for a special dispensation to sleep with another woman. People said he'd gone *wild* for a whore named Anne Boleyn. It was shocking stuff for an untouched country virgin like me.

Catherine's marriage was on secret trial that everybody knew about, and the king had not-so-secretly proposed to Anne. Those were seriously tense times. The court was awash with rumour, with spies and backstabbing and divided loyalties between the two queens of the court, Catherine and Anne. It was a snake pit.

But I kept my head down and my reputation clean. And it was fairly impressive, in those days, that I managed to make it through my time as lady-in-waiting to not one but two queens without a single rumour or flirtation.

Things calmed down for a while, when Henry finally banished my mistress, the kind and pious Queen Catherine, who never did a thing wrong in her life. But after Cranmer convened the court and hurriedly declared the marriage invalid, after the long years of fighting, Anne was crowned and Henry was excommunicated. And I went from lady-in-waiting to one wife, to another.

At that point, my brother and my father both sat up and took notice. One lady-in-waiting was now queen. Perhaps, in time, another lady-in-waiting could take her place on the throne.

So they invited the king. In September 1535, the royal progress stopped at Wolf Hall, which is where Henry first got a good look at me. He wasn't captivated—bear in mind he was still playing around with Anne Boleyn's cousin, Madge Shelton, then—but he did notice me. I looked better out of court, not competing with the great ladies in their fancy dresses and witty talk. I was humble, and sweet, and relentlessly domestic.

There was something quite sweet about him, too, you know. After he started going after me, he gave me a locket. Of course, inside it was a portrait of himself, which, I'll be honest, seemed an oddly narcissistic thing to do. Plus Anne ripped it off my neck. Everybody thought that was a big show of Anne's love and wild sexual jealousy, but I knew better. She was only trying to assert her own power. But Henry was still married to her—technically—as well as Queen Catherine—sort of. He wasn't about to propose again. Yet.

Then things began to move faster than you can imagine, when Anne's downfall began. I remember 1536 as the year of the three queens. Catherine, Anne, me. My former mistress, my still-beloved Catherine of Aragon, died in January. And suddenly Henry was technically a widower in most people's eyes.

But as soon as the news reached court, Anne—who was in and out of hot water—seemed to be back on the rise. The shadow over her marriage had cleared, and rightly or wrongly she was carrying the child they both hoped so much would be a son. She had a nerve, that one. I almost lost mine.

But soon people felt brave enough to start hinting that they knew what was going on between Henry and me. Trust me, nothing stays secret for long when it comes to sex and scandal.

Then poor Henry fell from his horse, and reopened the old jousting wound, and Anne lost the child from shock.

CATHERINE: *Actually, it was the day of my funeral that she miscarried. God's ways really are mysterious, aren't they?*

You're telling me!

But everything changed. She blamed her miscarriage on me, on my flirtation with the king—and may God have mercy on her for that. The truth is that after Anne had her miscarriage, the king wanted rid of her. I knew that, she knew that, and everybody knew it but him. It was just a question of how, and when.

That was my moment. And so, our courtship moved out into the open.

Henry switched his bedroom to one nearer me. He started visiting me every day, but as I was still an unmarried virgin—in my mid-twenties—I couldn't let him into my rooms. I refused to be a mistress. I held on to my virtue because it was all I bloody *had*, pardon the language. I didn't have the dowry of Catherine of Aragon or the wealth and lands he'd showered Anne with in their early days. I didn't have a bean, frankly. All I had was my reputation, and I wasn't about to give it up.

But, come on, I might have been a virgin, but I wasn't an idiot. I didn't do *nothing*. After all, the one thing I did learn from Anne was that a man does not marry his mistress, but he might wed a whore if she can hold out.

So I played a part. I did it for love, and at my family's urging, but I still played the modest maiden. I publicly rejected his gifts. "On my honour, sire, I could never accept this from a married man!" I blushed and simpered. I knew that deep down, under it all, he was still the kind of man who wanted to chase for love.

DID YOU KNOW?

- The time between my death and Henry's next marriage was his longest interval between his marriages—more than two years.

- My brother Thomas Seymour flirted with my stepdaughter Elizabeth and later married Henry's final wife, Catherine Parr. Both of my brothers were eventually executed.

- After my death, I continued to be painted into royal portraits as the king's consort.

- When Henry died, he was buried beside me in Windsor Castle.

I hinted at the country's feelings on his second marriage. That wasn't a ploy—I genuinely didn't hold with Anne's loose French ways or fiery reformist views. Her whole way of being, of talking, of dressing, even of *walking*, was foreign to me. Truth be told, I disapproved of her. Most of us did.

Cromwell himself gave me his apartments in Greenwich. Suddenly, I wasn't just the dull lady-in-waiting or just another Seymour child. As far as my brother Edward and my father were concerned, I was the meal ticket. And Henry used the back passages to those apartments and visited me every single day.

When Anne was arrested and disappeared from court one morning in May, my brother and Henry's friends quickly spirited me away to Sir Nicholas Carew's fancy house in Croydon, south London, which is still a great place to be off grid, so I'm told.

I didn't know much about what was happening in Anne's trial, but I did fear the worst for her. You see, when it was Queen Catherine's marriage on trial, they thought they could just push her aside quietly. But what they got was a seven-year fight, threats from abroad, and mutiny within court. They couldn't risk that a second time. Henry didn't need another ex-wife, particularly one as young as Anne. He needed a clean slate. Even after all that time, Catherine still had a hold on them both.

And I knew what Cromwell was like. I wasn't as clueless as everyone thought. I knew he'd dredge up the worst of the gossip, the dirtiest of the gutter talk, to paint a picture of a treasonous whore when all Anne really was, was a dreadful flirt and—let's just call it like it is—sexy.

I knew at least one of the charges was patently ridiculous. People were saying that Anne had been sleeping with Sir Henry Norris even when she had just given birth to Princess Elizabeth. She hadn't even been churched then, for God's sake! She was still unclean, messy with childbirth. There was simply *no way* she was having an affair then. Not someone as fastidious as her.

But the wicked men of the Church and of the court used vile gossip and slander like that to try her in the court of public opinion. And in those days, when you were accused of treason, you weren't allowed a defence. The four young men were sentenced to a cruel and inhumane death: they were hanged, drawn, and quartered. I don't know if you still have that punishment, but what that means is they were first dragged through the streets, then crucified almost to the point of death. Then they were cut down, disembowelled, castrated, and had their limbs quartered. It was, and I cannot stress it enough, a terrible way to die—not befitting of any of those young gentlemen.

Henry kept visiting me day in, day out, while Anne sat in that cold, damp Tower and waited to die. I never forgot that

DON'T L*o*SE YOUR HEAD

for a second, nor could I enjoy the attention of the most powerful man in the country while his wife—whatever her crimes, whatever the legitimacy of their marriage, but his *wife*, the mother of his child—looked out onto the grounds and watched them build her execution scaffold.

 ANNE: *Ha! All this sympathy, Jane. But I didn't see you come visit me.*

How could I? People thought me simple, but I was hardly such a ninny as to visit you in jail.

 ANNE: *True. But mon Dieu, all my passion to be replaced by a bland beige like you.*

Yes, well, that aside, Anne was still a problem. Who knows what she might say on the hour of her death? So Cromwell decided to keep her execution private. They said it was as a courtesy to her, but I knew better.

You see, opinion was divided. Anne, whom the people had hated so much that they spat at her in the streets, the witch who had seduced their beloved king and tried to kill their old Queen Catherine, was starting to gain pity. Honestly? Henry had made the people feel stupid. Woe betide a ruler who does that to his subjects. You can lie to the people, you can disregard the people, but you cannot make fools of them. Henry had torn the country apart for her, and now there we were just a few short years later, and he had thrown her aside.

Nobody knew what was going on. Was a young queen supposed to die for flirting with her courtiers? What kind of king was this? Those who had supported his getting rid of Catherine weren't happy to be made turncoats.

People mocked me, and I was scared. I wasn't a great royal princess of Europe; I wasn't a strong intellectual. I was just a simple farm girl at heart. I wanted to be married, but I didn't want to be queen. Not in its own right. What did I know of running a great house or navigating the political currents, of surfing the waves of favour and the religious disputes? I just wanted to garden in peace.

I don't know much about anything, really, but in my heart, I do know this: Anne didn't deserve to die. He could have sent her to a convent. He could have sent her into exile in France. He could have humbled her to dust. But he didn't have to kill her. And when he rushed to tell me the good news, that his beloved had been sentenced to death, it made me sick.

The poet Thomas Wyatt wrote that those bloody days broke his heart. What nobody knows is that they broke mine, too. Because I knew at that moment who I was marrying. And there wasn't a thing I could do about it.

DON'T LOSE YOUR HEAD

I knew who Henry was. I had watched him toss over one loyal wife in madness for another and then turn on her with the French sword. But I had sworn to love Henry 'til the end, and I stood by him. We were betrothed the very next day.

At least I got my way over the wedding. I wanted no great fuss, no solemn state occasion. It was simply too tasteless. We were married ten days later at the Palace of Whitehall. He did make a bit of a fuss of me when he brought me into the city on Whitsunday to introduce me to the people. I might have had my head turned by it had I been a different woman: all the velvet-coated men of the procession, the dancers, the streamers, the royal barge going up the river to the sound of trumpets.

 ANNE: *And my headless body was still warm in the ground.*

Look, Anne, you know my motto was "Bound to obey and serve." And that's what I did.

And hey, I got rich, too. I wasn't so altruistic, meek, and modest not to get excited by all the money and land that came with being queen. Not just for me, but for my family, too. And yes, I was *dripping* with jewels.

But I learnt. I kept my calm and temper where Anne had rained down fury. I never interfered where Catherine had influenced policy. I learnt from both of them. I never tried to be a queen or a rival to either. Instead, I focussed on what I knew best: how to run a home. I tightened things up in my household, banning all the loose French fashions that had taken hold in the walls of the court like weed creepers. People thought I was conservative, but really, I just wasn't stupid. Two ladies-in-waiting had taken the king from his wife. I wasn't about to let it happen a third time.

I did my duty: I focussed on the children. I pushed Henry to make up with his daughter Mary and restore her as his heir. Catherine Parr gets all the credit, but I began the process. The truth is, I liked her. We'd served together, and she was only seven years younger than me. I also wasn't so ignorant of my maternal fussing's effect on Henry. He liked me to look motherly. That was what he wanted.

Besides, I did feel for Mary, and for little Elizabeth, too. I mean, she was only four. Henry's second Act of Succession, which he passed that year, basically made both girls bastards, forcing them from their place in line to the throne for any children I might have. And when his bastard son, Henry Fitzroy, died that summer, I comforted him and gave him the news that I was carrying a legitimate son. But that poor boy's death broke Henry, and he was never the same again.

The *only* time I ever showed my true grit was when the great Northern men rose up against the reforms of the Church in the Pilgrimage of Grace. They hated Cranmer's changes, they hated the new Bible, and they hated the infringement of their Northern independence. And Henry was furious.

Inspired, I begged my husband to show mercy on them. In my heart I was still a good Catholic who *loathed* what he was doing to the abbeys. But Henry, with his piggy eyes and bloated face, looked me square in the eye and reminded me what had happened to the last woman who had "meddled in his affairs." That shut me up. I didn't criticise his religious policy again.

And he took women. Behind the haystacks. Behind trees. In the walled gardens of the palaces. Anywhere and everywhere he could have them, he did. He didn't show me the respect due to Catherine, princess of the blood, or to Anne, out of fear of her jealous temper. I wasn't an equal or an enchantment. I was just a womb. I think he was scared of what people were saying behind his back about his manhood, about his ability to make love to a woman. He wanted to prove all of them wrong.

Good thing that I was pregnant by Christmas—although our joy was short-lived and ended in an early, bloody miscarriage. That was when I started to really panic. All those dead babies of Catherine, all the miscarriages of Anne. Was the problem really Henry? That was a long, cold winter for me.

But I bounced back, hid my grief, and was pregnant again before he could turn against me. And in May, I felt our baby move in my stomach for the first time. Henry had never been more devoted. He treated me more like a queen, in those months, than ever before, although truth be told I was beginning to wear thin. What could I possibly use to entertain? My great wit and intellect? My knowledge of statesmanship or policy? My sexual prowess? I had none of it. I *bored* him. Even in bed, all I knew how to do was lie underneath him and gasp while he squashed me with his girth. He wanted me to straddle him like a horse, the way I'd once wriggled on his lap. He never let up.

At least my family was happy. My brother Edward, already wreathed in titles through my marriage, was made a Privy Councillor. Thomas, my other brother, was a gentleman of the Privy Chamber. My sister Elizabeth married Gregory Cromwell, Thomas's heir. They all did well.

But at least, under my gown and straining against my stomacher, was living proof that he wasn't impotent. That he was still a man. When he walked around with his hand on my pregnant stomach, he was basically showing off an erection. Even as we walked through a city that *reeked* of the rotting corpses of all the rebels he'd beheaded.

Henry was so pleased that he arranged for my coronation in October, after the prince arrived. And so he did. After a long, hot, highly uncomfortable summer, on a quiet afternoon in October my labour pains kicked in.

For three long days, I struggled to get that baby out. In Hampton Court Palace, I felt as if the ghosts of Catherine and Anne were watching me struggle as they had. I'd never known pain or suffering, and I had no way to cope with it. I knew that they'd cut him out of me and throw me on the scrap heap if there was ever any hint that his life might be in danger. One Tudor prince is worth any number of Tudor wives. I was *terrified*.

They say you forget the pain of childbirth. I'm not sure why they say it—maybe it's wishful thinking or just men talking—but I will say that it is so awful it's possible your mind literally cannot comprehend it afterward.

The blood and shit and vomit, the tearing and pain. I could never have imagined. I thought, Is this what I was bred for? Was this what I was meant to endure?

 CATHERINE: *I was there with you. I was watching over you. I took no pleasure in your pain.*

 **ANNE:** *I did, a bit.*

Even though you'd been through the same, Anne? Christ, I still only remember it in snapshots. The midwives stoking up the fires. Hanging onto the bedposts by torn sheets. Screaming until my throat was cut glass. I screamed for my mother, I cursed at my God. I'd never sworn in my entire life, but by the time they yanked that baby from between my legs, I was swearing like a sailor. I'd say those words must have been invented by a woman two days into labour.

And at the rude o'clock of two, on 12 October 1537, my son was born. And the country went wild. Finally, they had their true Tudor prince. The succession was safe. Henry had an heir. And I had a son.

When I held my baby, it was all worth it. I'd never, in my quiet little life, felt happier. I'd never hoped to be anyone, do anything. And there I was, holding the son and heir of Henry VIII. The son who he'd always wanted, the boy for whom he'd destroyed two wives. I'd done what he'd been trying to do for the best part of three decades. And I had my child. I'd never loved anything before. I'd had no passions to dedicate myself to, no great schemes or hot pursuits. Just me, and my baby. I held him just once, but it was enough to make it all worth it.

Things got a little hazy after that. I know he was christened a few days later, with my beloved stepdaughter Mary as godmother and little Elizabeth in my brother Thomas's arms. That was a little ironic, given that Thomas would end up trying to marry Elizabeth—the fool.

My son was named Edward, born on the eve of Saint Edward's Day. I know people came to visit me in the chapel after the christening. I remember my brothers' glee as

DON'T LOSE YOUR HEAD

the family was showered in riches and lands and endless swag. I remember the warmth of my confinement room. I remember when it turned into heat and fever. I don't remember much after that, only that less than a fortnight later, I was dead. I was only twenty-eight.

Henry, they say, was so heartbroken that he shut himself off from the world with just his fool, Will Somers. Henry wore black for three months, my gaudy magpie of a husband who so loved bright colours and Lincoln green. He called me a phoenix, dying in a fire to give birth to another.

 ANNE: *He still kept your dowry, though.*

Well, yeah. I mean, he was still greedy. He stuffed himself with food to feed the emptiness he couldn't face. He made himself sick, bloated, obese.

And as the years went by, he began to idolise me more and more. That quiet little woman whom he never really knew. The wisdom of hindsight? Or a rose-tinted baby view of the past? Presumably I shone only in comparison to what came after. Don't it always seem to go, that you don't know what you got 'til it's died in childbirth.

But the Tudor court is no place for sentimentality, and his councillors began the search for another wife before I was even in the ground. Though that's another woman's tale to tell.

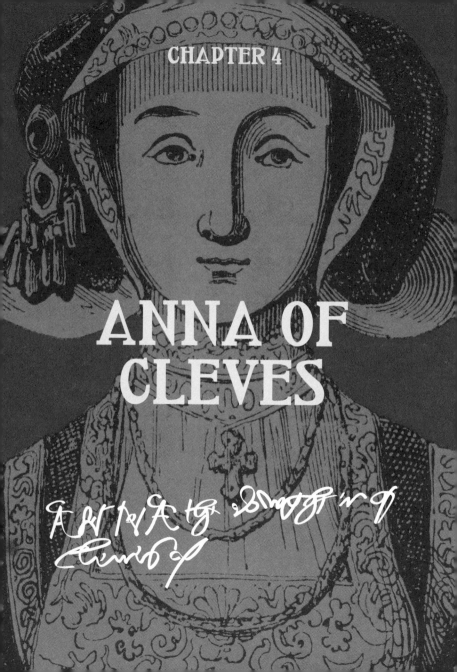

CHAPTER 4

ANNA OF CLEVES

PROFILE

NAME: Anna of Cleves / Anna von Kleve, also spelled Anne

OTHER TITLES: The King's Beloved Sister

BORN: 22 September or 28 June 1515 in Dusseldorf, Germany

PARENTS: John III of the House of La Marck, Duke of Cleves, and Maria, Duchess of Jülich-Berg

NOTABLE ANCESTORS: House of La Marck

SIBLINGS: Sybilla (born 1512), William (born 1516), Amelia (born 1517)

CHILDHOOD: Grew up in Burg Castle, Solingen (north-western Germany), was engaged at age eleven

LOOKS: Long fair hair, heavy eyes, clear skin, rosy cheeks, curvy

PERSONALITY: Calm, generous, confident, pleasant, self-indulgent, a good boss

EDUCATION: Not much formal education but could read and write in German, was good at needlework

RELIGION: Born a Catholic; converted to Anglican Protestant in England

MARRIAGES:

- Francis, heir to Antoine, Duke of Lorraine (betrothed): 5 June 1527, canceled 1535
- Henry VIII: 6 January 1540, age twenty-four

AGE DIFFERENCE WITH HENRY: Twenty-three years

MOTTO: "God send me well to keep"

MARRIAGE ENDED: 9 July 1540, after six months, annulled because of previous betrothal to Francis

DIED: 16 July 1557 at Chelsea Old Manor, age forty-one, most likely of cancer

BURIED: Westminster Abbey, near Edward the Confessor's shrine

DID YOU KNOW?

I was first suggested as a bride for Henry in 1533—years before he married Anne Boleyn.

My brother was also suggested for Henry's daughter, Princess Mary.

Hans Holbein the Younger painted my portrait in Düren, as well as that of my sister Amelia, who was also being considered as a bride. My painting is now in the Louvre.

DON'T LOSE YOUR HEAD

You know, I was never really divorced, either. And how is it that Catherine Parr is the one they say survived? Joke's on her; I survived long after she did.

I'm the one you know least about. The *Hausfrau*, the great Flanders mare, the ugly one. *Ach so*, how is it that I ended up one of the richest, most powerful women in the country? The king's beloved sister, no less. With no man to tie me down or tell me what to do. A bed to myself and wealth to boot.

They called me dull-witted. A stolid buffoon. Plain and stupid. So stupid, *ja*, that I was the one who ended up with all the money and freedom. And I outlived them all. My motto was "God send me well to keep." And that's exactly what He did.

Schatzi, you might know the least about me, but I know the most about everyone else. I knew Jane Seymour's son. I was close with Catherine of Aragon's daughter. I was stepmother to Henry's three children long after all the other wives. I lived long enough to see Prince Edward crowned, to see Princess Mary married to Philip of Spain and crowned in Westminster Abbey. I retired to Chelsea Old Manor, Catherine Parr's house. I used her privy after she was dead. You can probably tell I was no fan of hers.

> **CATHERINE PARR:** *Go figure. I wasn't too keen on you, either.*

So how did I do it? How did a little German girl, an uneducated peasant in their eyes, end up with the biggest prize? How did I manage to be Queen of England for just six months but the king's sister for the rest of my life?

To understand how I did it, you have to know why I was there in the first place—and what I didn't start with that the other wives did.

DID YOU KNOW?

- I wasn't technically divorced. My marriage was declared unconsummated, which means Henry told everyone that he had never managed to have sex with me.

- After our wedding night, Henry told his friends that he didn't think I was a virgin.

- My brother did not send the documents that proved that my previous betrothal had been revoked, so Henry could use that against me.

My father, John III, was Duke of Cleves, and my mother, Maria, was heiress to the duchies of Jülich and Berg.

When they married, they united the three into one, in a northwestern wet bit of what you'd now know as Germany. I was born in the capital, Düsseldorf, in a castle called Schloss Burg.

I wasn't much to look at: the middle daughter between Miss Perfect, Sybilla, and the precious baby Amelia. And, of course, the one who mattered, my younger brother, William—the heir. But I had a good name: Anna von Jülich-Kleve-Berg. Or, as you probably know me, Anna of Cleves. My family had some impressive ancestors, like the house of La Marck, but we were fairly humble. I still had that all-important drop of royal blood, though.

I spent most of my childhood in Castle Burg, a glorified mountaintop lodge with great views of the river Wupper. The duchy of Cleves wasn't much to look at, but it was pretty strategically important.

I stayed by my mother's side. She taught me everything she thought I needed to know—how to sew, how to read and write in German, how to pray like a good Catholic. She was strict, you know, and I wasn't allowed any nonsense. We were dressed up like monks and taught to behave like nuns. I was well cared for but not well loved or educated, and I definitely didn't have any fun.

The religion side of things was pretty confusing. My mother might have been a strict Catholic, but my father was sympathetic to Erasmus, even though he thought Luther was talking nonsense. Our family motto was *"Candida nostra fides"* ("Our faith is honest").

My father corresponded with humanist scholars and put through Erasmian reforms to the Church. He banned parties and drinking. Parents, take note. If you withhold wine from your kids, you make it more attractive. Of course I was drawn to the hedonistic excess of the English courts.

When I was just eleven, my elder sister, Sybilla, married John Frederick of Saxony. They became religious reformers. She looked so beautiful that day, and I felt lost. Would I ever be as pretty? Would I have as good a marriage? Would she ever come back and visit?

But that same year, I became engaged to Francis, Duke of Bar, heir to the Duchy of Lorraine. My father agreed that Francis would become his heir. That annoyed my brother, William, no end.

So we signed the marriage contract, but we never even met. That was right around the time that the whole of Europe was up in arms over the King of England, Henry VIII, trying to get rid of his first wife on the (shaky) grounds that she had been married to his brother. Heirs and marriage contracts were taken pretty seriously. I don't remember much about it, but I do remember being warned over and over that a woman who cannot produce a son is a wife who can be thrown over for a younger model. Catherine of

Aragon haunted my childhood just as she would go on to haunt my marriage.

 ANNE: *Are you serious right now? She haunted your marriage?*

Well, so did you, to be fair. I was always going to be the other Anne, after you. Why do you think I go by Anna?

So anyway, there I was, engaged to a boy when I was just eleven. Francis was only nine, so the contract was *de futura*—a promise to get married in the future. And here's the strangest part of my story. It wasn't long after that the English courts were considering an alliance with Cleves, in case of war with France or Spain. Sybilla was married, so no good. William might have done for Princess Mary, but Amelia was still too young.

It was my brother, William, who was the problem. Again. That's going to be a feature in this story.

My sister got involved in the Schmalkaldic League, a team of Lutheran princes who swore that they would never go back to the Catholic Church. Her husband was the head of it. He was pretty friendly with Luther, actually.

So there I was. I spent each summer in Swan Castle, another of our family houses, waiting for my swan-knight, and each wet winter watching the rain tickle the rivers. My elder sister was doing important things, my younger sister was adorable, my brother was shaping himself up to be a puffed-up princeling. And I was having dinner with my mother every night listening to lectures on religious decorum, with no chance to dance or feast or make merry at all. My most fertile years were flying by, and I couldn't even drink.

But when my brother, William, took over for my father and became duke, he snatched up the duchy of Guelders after Charles of Egmond died. Guess who was heir to Gelderland? My betrothed, Francis.

If I had gone ahead with my betrothal, I'd have inherited the lot. So my brother ruined my marriage out of spite. And suddenly I was back on the marriage menu.

And then things started to change quickly. In 1536, Queen Catherine of Aragon died, and the Catholics lost a step. Then King Henry set fire to the papish idols and the monasteries. He turned on Anne Boleyn, the reformer, and the Erasmians lost a step. His new wife, an English snore by the name of Jane, was down the aisle and up the casket before you could say *nonentity*.

 JANE: *Easy, tiger, I was queen for longer than you. And I gave him his only legitimate heir.*

Are you going to hold on to that one forever?

King Henry was looking for a wife again, but he was hardly a catch: no longer the athletic young man but a fat, aging grump with a vile temper. And there was a rush: he was only getting older. Of course, had he been a woman, he would've been far off the shelf. His ulcerous leg was getting worse; he was putting on weight like a pig for slaughter. He couldn't play sports, or even barely walk, and the wound stank of rotting pus.

He also had a baby prince in the nursery, part of one of the most powerful families in the country, and two princesses both cast aside, and nobody knew what was going to happen next. Would it be another English lady-in-waiting? A French whore? A Portuguese princess?

But marrying Henry would still have been a great coup for a princess in Europe. And while Francis I of France and Charles V of the Holy Roman Empire were playing tug-of-war, Henry needed some ammo. And what did Francis and Charles have in common? They were both Catholic. And my brother was aligned with the Lutheran protestants.

Enter me, the one nobody saw coming.

So why *did* they put me forward? Why a German *Fräulein* rather than another English rose? After Anne Boleyn's French fire and Jane Seymour's English beige, did he need something a little different? A Lutheran bride, a strict Erasmian virgin, a sensible girl?

I couldn't sing. I couldn't dance. I didn't know much about music, for all that Cleves had had an orchestra. I couldn't turn a witty phrase in Latin. I couldn't even speak English.

It all starts and ends with Thomas Cromwell, a young man rising up the ranks of Cardinal Wolsey's household to become his secretary. By 1532, he was chief minister. He had brought down Catherine of Aragon with his intelligence. He took down Anne Boleyn, his former ally. He was a reformer, and ambitious as hell. And when Francis of France and Charles of Spain signed the Truce of Nice, a ten-year agreement without any mention of England, something had to be done.

So Cromwell, that wily dog, decided to combine the need for a strong front against the Catholic kingdoms with his own desire for reform. He invited some ambassadors to discuss the Schmalkaldic League. He was pretty keen on us Germans, actually.

And things in England were getting worse by the month. Henry's paranoia about his succession was out of control, and he was murdering anybody too close to his bloodline. The Pope was threatening to excommunicate him, and everybody was afraid.

Meanwhile, Holbein was sent all over Europe to paint portraits of eligible women. But one by one, they made their excuses. One became a nun. Another played sick. Everybody knew by then that Henry wasn't exactly the golden prince, the flower of the Tudors, anymore. He was old, for God's sake. His health was failing, and he wasn't exactly known for being a great husband, no matter what some later historians might say.

So then there were three of us in the mix: Christina of Denmark. She was only a teenager but already a widow, and the niece of Charles V. Very beautiful, married at thirteen to Francesco Sforza, Duke of Milan. He was twenty-six years older, so she wouldn't be bothered by a massive age difference. They didn't bank on her sassiness. She said she didn't trust him or his council because she suspected that he had poisoned Catherine of Aragon. And who was that? Christina's great-aunt, of course.

And then there were my sister Amelia and me. I was no great beauty, but I was good on paper. I was twenty-four, unmarried, and the sister of the new Duke of Cleves, who was a good ally against Rome. Plus, it wouldn't make sense to take the younger sister. Would it?

I wasn't as stupid as they thought. To a strict little virgin like me, Henry wasn't an appealing prospect. But I knew that this was my chance. I knew that being Queen of England, even under someone like Henry VIII, would be better than being left the unwanted spinster in Cleves. Of course, I'd end up an unwanted spinster anyway, but at least I would be rich in England and able to do whatever I wanted. In

Cleves, there was always my mother to scold me or my brother to dominate. And I needed to get out.

I want you to imagine what it felt like. To be painted by Holbein. To know that your entire future depends on the whim of one man's interpretation of your nose. Your complexion, the lighting. Bound up in fustian and strapped up tighter than an unruly horse. It's hot, and you can't breathe properly. The sweat is dripping down your back, and the boning of your corset is biting into your ribs.

I want you to imagine, if you can, the fear of the shame, which is almost always worse than shame itself. How it would feel to be passed over for the younger daughter, to miss your turn, the middle child, the unwanted heifer.

And d'you know what? For all that they said later that I looked nothing like my portrait, that's a lot of *Scheisse*. I looked *exactly* like my portrait. I might not have been a great beauty, but I had long fair hair, good clear skin, and big, expressive eyes. I lacked the poise of Catherine of Aragon, the flare of Anne Boleyn, and the serenity of Jane Seymour. But those were not what he wanted.

He'd had his passions, he'd had his loves and his queens. He'd had what he always wanted: a Tudor prince in the cradle. Now he just needed a solid match. Someone useful with whom he could make a last alliance. A sturdy bet to take over the running of the nursery, to mind the heir and maybe push out a spare. Henry wasn't looking for a great love when he looked into the eyes of my portrait and tried to imagine how we'd get on.

So when he said he rejected me because I wasn't *pretty* enough? *Ach so*, what complete baloney.

In fact, it was Christina's portrait he'd really gone mad for. Even so, his advisers were pretty stupid. They were looking at it from a purely political stance. They forgot that Henry liked to fall in love. And in my case, there wasn't even a suggestion of love, courtly or otherwise.

DID YOU KNOW?

- My last appearance as Henry's wife was at the May Day celebrations. Just like Anne Boleyn.

- I outlived all the other queens—Catherine Parr by nine years—and lived to see his daughter Mary crowned Queen Mary I. I played a major part in her coronation.

- I was rumoured to have had a secret child with Henry in November 1541. The Privy Council took this rumour very seriously.

- I was known for loving a good glass of wine. They say the freedom of being a rich singleton went to my head.

But anyway, he took me, in the end. My family insisted that the betrothal to Francis was no issue, and the marriage treaty was signed on 4 October 1539. I should have gotten over there fast, by sea, but just the idea of it frightened the hell out of me. None of us knew how impatient Henry was and how stupid it would be to make him wait past Christmas.

After a gruelling overland journey, I arrived in England: a totally new world. I felt like a fat cow in my stupid German clothes, from a little Lutheran court of Nowheresville, while the English ladies swanned around in their elegant dresses and their necks out. I was all alone in a country that wasn't exactly keen for a new queen. That said, despite my lack of graces, I did manage to impress everyone with my manners and gentleness. I made a good impression on them, at least. Not so my new husband.

Perhaps if I had known Henry, known his ways, things wouldn't have gone down as they did on that New Year's Day in Rochester. The first day of 1540. Because unlike the three wives before me, I didn't have the luxury of years with Henry. No letters, no words, no stolen caresses, and no intellectual sparring. I knew nothing about his massive ego. I didn't know that he liked to play dress-up and to not be recognised. I didn't have a clue, actually. And nobody told me.

He didn't have a clue, either. Remember, he'd known all his first three wives before he married them. So I was the unknown delivery from abroad, and Henry liked to let his imagination run wild. While we were still on our journey from Dover, we stopped at Rochester Abbey to rest on New Year's Day. And Henry's patience in waiting for me finally gave way. He decided to come get me. In his head, he was still the handsome, lusty young prince who had ridden to the rescue of Catherine of Aragon and who had risked it all for love for Anne and Jane.

He and his gentlemen rode to Rochester in brightly coloured cloaks as disguises. I was watching the bullbaiting through the window and was totally taken off my guard when what I thought was a stranger burst into the room. He stormed over to me and grabbed me around the waist, and before I could even slam my mouth shut he'd suckered his stinking mouth onto mine.

Imagine—that was the first time a man had even touched me. How would you have felt? If any man is reading this, I want him to remember that the buildup to the kiss is everything. You've got to give us time to duck, at least.

The arrogance of that *Dummkopf*. He might have gotten away with dressing up as Robin of the Forest, or whoever it was, when he was young and handsome and Catherine of Aragon was an indulgent mother-wife. How could he possibly have thought that would work with me?

So I was shocked, and disgusted, and afraid, and angry. I thought he was just some fat old beggar. I had no idea that I had just spat out the kiss of my husband-to-be. All these years later, and it still makes me cringe.

And even though he came back in later, all done up properly to look like a king, the damage was done. First impressions are pretty important, you know. He told Cromwell that he couldn't like me, that I wasn't as pretty as people had said.

Jawohl, the feeling was mutual. They were still calling him the golden prince! And here he was, limping on his rotten leg, a swollen boil with decaying teeth and barely any hair left to call golden. He saw, in that moment, in my face, who he really was to women now, and he hated me for it. He was going to be rid of me, no matter how useful I was. And he was going to find someone to blame.

Why did they even let it happen? Cromwell persuaded Henry that to reject me outright would enrage Cleves, the last ally in Europe, which would cause huge trouble for his foreign policy.

Cromwell couldn't get the king out of the marriage, so Cromwell had to go. But I could. You see, my people from Cleves were supposed to bring a document that proved that my betrothal to Francis had been set aside. That all-important dispensation. And when Henry went looking for a reason to be rid of me, he went with what had worked before, with Catherine of Aragon: that I was pre-contracted to another man. The Cleves ambassadors swore they'd get the papers to him but that it could take weeks. Henry's hands were tied.

And I arrived in London to meet my people. They were weirdly excited by another exotic foreign bride. And so we were married, on Blackheath outside Greenwich Park, by Archbishop Thomas Cranmer. And even though as a bride I dressed in a gold gown with jewels in my hair, and looked my very best, it wasn't enough. It was a proper royal wedding, with all the state and pomp. Perhaps if that had been our first meeting, everything would have been different. But there's no point in thinking like that now.

Hours after our wedding, Henry was back with his Privy Council, demanding a way out. But, of course, he still had to have his wedding night.

So there we were, alone at last. He the seasoned groom of forty-eight, a man who had already had every possible woman every which way. A man who could barely move, who had to be hoofed into my bed like a hayball. A man whose leg wound ran stinking pus. And there was me, a twenty-four-year-old virgin. I'd barely ever seen a man, let alone been in a bed with one. And I might have known what to do, but I certainly didn't know how to encourage.

No big surprise that after our first night together, Henry told Cromwell that he liked me even less. He said that I was fat, with saggy breasts. He said that I smelled. He said that

I was no virgin. But he also said that he couldn't do it with me. He tried every night, for four nights, to do it. But after that, he never tried again. He kissed me goodnight every night and good morning every morning, and nothing in between.

I played the innocent to my ladies. I pretended that I had no knowledge of the birds and the bees, that I didn't know what was expected of me as a royal bride. But if you believe that, you're as stupid as Henry. Because that was the only thing that I'd been bred for. I was just trying to protect my honour, and his pride. I needn't have bothered, really.

It sounds odd to say, but despite all those insults, he didn't really blame me. How could he? I was just a sexless mare to him. He blamed Cromwell. A man like Henry will always blame the giver of the gift he rejects. I was the toy he chucked out of the pram: Cromwell was the idiot pushing the pram.

Trust me, the portrait wasn't the problem. How could it have been? It's not as if Holbein fell out of favour, did he? Besides, Henry may have been a lot of things, but he wasn't stupid. Nobody was going to buy that.

The real truth? He was still a romantic fool. He wanted to feel Cupid's arrow. He wanted another Anne to make him feel young, a Catherine to make him feel loved, a Jane to make him feel blessed. Cromwell accounted for politics, but he never considered passion. Henry was a man of unbridled appetite by that point, a binge-eater of distraction.

And he had already turned his piggy little eyes to another. My maid, Katherine "Kitty" Howard, a mere slip of a thing, a silly little flirt. A seventeen-year-old child. And not so chaste, if you're to believe everything you hear.

KATHERINE: *Now just hold on a second, Lady Anna. I was a good servant to you. You know that I had nothing to do with it. The king had already put you aside by the time he came to me.*

All I know is, I ended up with the prize and you ended up on a block.

KATHERINE: *What was I supposed to do?*

You? What about *me?!* You played the innocent little girl, but you had powerful allies. Your uncle was the Duke of Norfolk. You were of the Howard family, cousin to the Boleyns. You might not have been worth a damn to anyone in and of yourself, but you were a pretty little pawn. Norfolk was Cromwell's enemy.

Okay, I'm being unfair. It wasn't her fault. But when the France-Spain alliance inevitably began to crack, Henry saw his chance at freedom from me and a chance at possessing Kitty. And Cromwell couldn't give him what he wanted.

I liked it in England, you know. I liked my new clothes, the music, the dancing, the drinking, the *fun*. I liked playing with my toddler stepson, Prince Edward, the little Princess Elizabeth.

When my brother, once again, failed to send the documents that would prove my betrothal to Francis was over, Henry saw his way out. He kept Cromwell just long enough to tell Parliament that the king's marriage was invalid, and then he arrested him. To be honest, I'm not sure Henry had ever forgiven Cromwell for the part he'd played in the marriage with Anne.

He sent me to Richmond Palace, in exile. And soon his envoys came to ask for my consent to annul the marriage. And unlike Catherine of Aragon, I gave it. I said yes where she said no. I swore I'd cause no trouble, that it was all my own fault. Because, girls, if he's risking foreign policy and invasion and executing his people to get rid of you, maybe *he's just not that into you*.

So I let him go, and I let him think it was his idea. I even told my brother, forced to dictate the letter under their watchful eye, why I'd been rejected. I promised to be a good, humble servant and not to make a fuss. I took every bit of humiliation he threw at me and turned it into triumph.

I blossomed, after just six months with a madman. Because one woman's exile is another woman's freedom.

Catherine might have been sure of her place in Heaven, but I got the castles. Richmond Palace, and Hever Castle. Ironically, that was where Anne Boleyn grew up. Henry was so pleased with my giving him a way out that he gave me the title of the King's Beloved Sister and said I would take precedence over every woman in the kingdom, behind his new wife and daughters.

Ah yes, his new wife. And what of her, little Katherine Howard, my silly maid? Henry married Katherine just nineteen days after our marriage ended. He executed Cromwell on the very same morning. What kind of man does that?

A lot of people thought I spent the rest of my days out there in my palaces, swigging my wine, but the truth is less juicy. I spent many, many years toeing the line warily. I came back to court while Katherine, the child queen, was on the throne. I swallowed my pride and curtsied to my former servant.

I didn't blame her. And truth be told, I felt sorry for her. She was just a child, really. And now Henry had no Wolsey, no Cromwell, no Catherine of Aragon, and no Anne Boleyn. All the people who could advise him or control him were gone. He trusted no one.

Once that man, my ex-husband, took a young girl and sliced her head off, none of us were ever safe again. That was the moment. That was the moment when everyone in the country knew what their golden prince had become: a tyrant king, a killer of children. He might have persuaded a lot of people that Anne Boleyn deserved to die, but nobody thought the same of Katherine Howard.

DID YOU KNOW?

- My sister Sybilla and her husband, John Frederick of Saxony, looked after one of Germany's biggest libraries, where Martin Luther sheltered after his 95 Theses caused a stir. John Frederick even got him out of town after the Holy Roman Emperor Charles V denounced him.

- I never returned to my homeland, staying in England all my life.

- I was the only one of the six to be given a burial in Westminster Abbey.

- My monument has the earliest example of skull and crossbones ever recorded in England.

So all we could do after that was keep our heads down and hope for better days as the religious debates turned into civil turmoil and Henry grew closer and closer to death.

DON'T LOSE YOUR HEAD

After Katherine died, there were many times when I was suggested again as a bride for Henry, but I sidestepped the lot of them. I focussed on being a stepmother to the three royal children.

My Cleves brethren were pushing the reconciliation, but where had they been when he was throwing me aside for my teenage maid?

So I kept my head down, and he went to the widow Catherine Parr instead. I lived long enough to watch her die, too, trying to give birth to a child for a man who was more interested in diddling our stepdaughter. But I suppose that's her story to tell.

Everything has its price, though. I might have been comfortable, but I never went home. I never married; I never had children. I'm not sure Henry even realised what he'd done by asking me to agree that I was pre-contracted. It means he was condemning me to a childless life as a virgin spinster. But I knew what I was sacrificing when I agreed. And at least I had my stepchildren.

What I didn't know, what I *couldn't* have known, is what would happen to Kitty. His wrath fell on her like a tonne of bricks. And she might have had a powerful family, but she also had the stink of Boleyn on her. She wasn't a great lady of Europe. She wasn't nobility. She was just a child.

But let her tell it. I'm off back to my palace.

CHAPTER 5

KATHERINE HOWARD

PROFILE

NAME: Katherine Howard, also known as Kitty

BORN: 1521–1523 (?) in Lambeth, London

PARENTS: Lord Edmund Howard and Joyce Culpeper

NOTABLE ANCESTORS: Elizabeth Howard (Katherine's aunt and mother of Anne Boleyn); Thomas Howard, 2nd Duke of Norfolk

SIBLINGS: Five, and six half-siblings from her mother's first marriage

CHILDHOOD: Was sent to live with her father's stepmother in Norfolk after her mother's death; grew up in Norfolk House (Lambeth) and Chesworth House (Sussex) with other wards

LOOKS: Blonde-red hair, hooked Howard nose, very slim, fresh-faced

PERSONALITY: Lively, jocular, flirtatious, animal lover, capricious, passionate

EDUCATION: Literate but not educated; excellent dancer

RELIGION: Roman Catholic

MARRIAGE: Henry VIII on 28 July 1540 at Oatlands Palace, Surrey; made public 8 August 1540, age about seventeen

AGE DIFFERENCE WITH HENRY: Thirty-two (?) years

MOTTO: "No other will but his"

MARRIAGE ENDED: 23 November 1541, when Archbishop Cranmer denounced her sexual past and accused her of concealing her unchastity and adultery

DIED: 13 February 1542, beheaded at the Tower of London

BURIED: Unmarked grave in Chapel Royal of St Peter ad Vincula, same as Anne Boleyn

DID YOU KNOW?

- I was cousins with Anne Boleyn, so I was the second Howard girl on the throne.

- When I was a young teenager, my music teacher abused and groomed me for two years. I also had a relationship with Francis Dereham, who considered me his wife. Both of those could be seen as rape.

- Henry married me just nineteen days after he annulled his marriage to Anna of Cleves. I was only seventeen.

- I was Henry's third wife to be a member of the English nobility.

- Henry found out about my affair with Thomas Culpeper from a love letter I wrote.

They call me the least relevant Katherine. Not even the most important Howard. The naughty child. The lewd girl queen. The flirt. The rose without a thorn. They never call me what I am: a victim. Lewd and naughty, the King of France called me. He wrote to Henry, you know, the day after I had my head cut off.

Everyone you've heard from so far—Catherine of Aragon, the great Spanish Queen; my cousin Anne Boleyn, the French courtier; Jane Seymour, the English saint; and my mistress, Anna of Cleves—they all had what I never had. A chance. They had families, friends, education, power in their own right. Clever adult women, all of them. Even Jane, who they say was a bit of a tit.

But I was just a child when the most powerful men in the country put me in the king's bed. And when he turned against me, I had nobody to run to. I was queen far longer than Jane Seymour or Anna of Cleves, but it took him only days to get rid of me.

 ANNA: *Er, excuse me? You were from one of the most powerful families in the country? The Howards!*

I was, and I wasn't. I was a Howard girl, but there were loads of us. They could have taken their pick of pretty little Howard girls to put in the king's bed. My parents weren't around, and my uncle, the Duke of Norfolk, couldn't have cared less. He'd had his chance of a niece on the throne with Anne. I was nowhere *near* as sophisticated as her.

Jane doesn't get it. The Seymours were also one of the most powerful families in the country—more so after she died, being family to Prince Edward. She had her brothers and her father taking care of her. And she died in childbirth. I'm sorry for her, of course I am, but it's not as if she was murdered.

People forget, you know. They forget that Anne's wasn't the only Howard head he chopped off. And when that blade came down, all those men congratulated themselves on a job well done. They blamed me for my affair with my beloved Thomas Culpeper. I don't know whether they ever realised that my death was all their fault.

I was born somewhere in the early 1520s, and I'm not even sure where. Lambeth, maybe? So when everything happened at court between Catherine of Aragon, Anne, and Jane, I was just a child and far away.

My aunt, my father's sister Elizabeth Howard, was Anne Boleyn's mother. So I was her first cousin.

My great-grandmother, Elizabeth Tilney, was the sister of Seymour's great-grandmother, Anne Say. So Jane and I were second cousins. Are you with me? So yeah, it sounds as if I came from money.

But think about it. My father, Lord Edmund Howard, was one of twenty-one children—the third son, no less. He hadn't a chamber pot to piss in. My mother, Joyce Culpeper (yes, a relation, but not that close), already had five children from Ralph Leigh, her first husband. Then she had another six with my father.

So I was the tenth child, or thereabouts. The spare of the spare of the spare. My mother died when I was just a little girl, and I was sent to live with the Dowager Duchess of Norfolk, my father's stepmother and my stepgrandmother, who had dozens of unwanted wards from aristocratic families down on their luck.

And that was where the fun began. Or trouble, depending on how you look at it. God, but it was *wild*. Just imagine: all of us kids, spare children of aristocrats with better things to do than parents, running free through the huge halls of Chesworth House in Sussex and Norfolk House in Lambeth.

For sure, the Dowager Duchess was strict, but she was almost never there. And there were more than a hundred of us in the household. We had food, we had shelter, we had pretty clothes and hardly any school. And most of all, we had boys. I and the other girls all bunked together with maids, and every night the young men of the household would sneak in. They brought food and wine and sang at our doors, pretending to call on us like lovesick swains from the stories of court. We would fall about laughing and drag them inside, theatrically hushing each other's giggles as we tumbled them into our warm beds. I saw everything that happened between boy and girl. When older ladies talked of virtue and chastity, I didn't really understand. I thought they meant to keep clean and tidy. So what did you expect would happen, Grandmama?

I met my own. Henry Mannox. I must have been what, thirteen? A child in your world but a flower ready to be plucked in mine. He was a grown man, about twenty-three, and they brought him in to teach me to play the lute. What were they thinking? He was a handsome young man, and I'd been brought up in the maids' quarter. I knew how to flirt, how to tease and titillate. What I didn't know how to do was stop it when things went too far for me. He was a neighbour to Chesworth house, and they brought him inside like a fox into a coop of juicy chickens.

While I practised my strings, he would come up behind me and lift my hair from the nape of my neck, stroke me, and kiss me. He would show me the strings on my arm, the proper hand movement on my thighs. He put his hands under my gown, under my shift, and caressed my stomacher. He touched me where I knew he wasn't really supposed to. And all the while he whispered in my ear that he loved me; that I was his little sweetheart. How was I to know any different? It went on for years. He followed me back to London, to the Lambeth House.

Of course, we were discovered. Things might have been lax around there, but I was hardly discreet. I'd told my girlfriends, half giggling, half ashamed, wanting to know if it was normal, whether we were really in love, whether I could keep my virtue and turn him down. Servants heard things in the hallway, they peeped around half-open doors, and the Dowager Duchess eventually found out. We were both hauled in for questioning. Jesus, I was terrified. But he admitted nothing. He said that I had tempted him like a snake. Not sure why he had to bring animals into it, but apparently it was something about the Bible. And I never saw him again.

You'd think I would have been sad, that I would have missed him, but I didn't. Truthfully, it had gone too far, and he wasn't a suitable husband for me anyway. I was young and alive, and I knew of love for the first time, but I wanted to aim higher. And why shouldn't I? I was pretty, I was fun, I knew how to flirt. Sure, I couldn't read or write, but I had golden hair and perfect skin, and I could dance like an Italian whore. But all the lectures and scolding over Henry had taught me one thing: that I was worth more. I was a Howard girl, of good breeding. I had no money, but I had my family, and I had my looks, and I could aim higher than a fumble with a lute player.

So when the Dowager Duchess's secretary, Francis Dereham, started after me, I thought it was my chance. God, but I loved him. There's truly nothing like a first love. I was *obsessed*. Even the smell of him would make me feel faint. I would look for him at every Mass, at every meal. I thought we were in love, wholly and purely like two carefree teenagers.

DID YOU KNOW?

- Culpeper and Dereham were both beheaded. Their heads were put on spikes on London Bridge. I passed under them on my way to the Tower.

- I was so distraught after my interrogation by Archbishop Cranmer that he removed anything I could use to kill myself.

- I had the block brought into my chamber the night before my execution to practise on it.

- After I was executed, my own family removed my picture from the portrait gallery. There is no painting in the world that is definitely of me.

- My ghost is said to haunt Hampton Court Palace.

He told me that I was his wife. We were playing house, he giving me his money to manage and I darning his shirts.

Well, I kept them under my pillow, anyway. Life's too short to darn. He told me that I belonged to him, that I had to do whatever he said. I thought it was the real thing. And when he told me I had to come to his bed as his wife, I believed him. But I was just a child.

It's easy enough to call me wife and sneak into my bed at night. It's much harder to go about things the right and proper way. He never put his money where his mouth was. He never went to my grandmother and asked for my hand. He never proposed. We might have been husband and wife at night, but he barely acknowledged me in the day. He called it forbidden love, secret, passionate, exciting. But it was bullshit. It was all play, in the end. He went off to Ireland, and I was left without a ring. And Mannox, a typical jealous snitch, told my grandmother everything. In an anonymous note, no less. I swore I'd never write anything that I was too cowardly to sign. Of course, that came back to haunt me…

But as far as my grandmother was concerned, I was spoiled. Trouble. And I was still just a teenager. But I had some value, in her mind. I was still pretty. I knew how to play a lute and please a man. What more did I need? And so it was off to court for me. And I had new gowns and hoods and a cape trimmed with fur. And I was happy to go.

My uncle, the Duke of Norfolk, wanted someone in the queen's rooms. He wasn't best pleased with Anna of Cleves as his queen, you see. I think it might have been because she was a Lutheran, or something? Certainly not for the old ways, like us sensible folk.

But when I got to court, I could see the real reason. It was because she was *boring*. She couldn't dance. She couldn't sing. She couldn't dress properly, all bound up like a dumpy German barrel. She couldn't even speak English, for God's sake! Who comes to the English court without any knowledge of the language? How did she expect to please the king like that, she who only ever got down on her knees to pray?

 ANNA: *Mind your tongue, Kitty. I'm still your mistress.*

I'm sorry, Your Grace. You know I grew to love you. But it's true: you weren't exactly a merry queen.

 ANNA: *Well, I'm merrier than you now. Swings and roundabouts.*

That's true. But he turned away from her and turned to me, waiting in the wings.

I wasn't all that clever, and I wasn't a great beauty, either. But I was young and fresh, and I was silly enough to seem witty compared with Anna. Henry was dazzled with me. I suppose compared with his lumpy wife, any country maid

 DON'T LOSE YOUR HEAD

would have done, but I think the truth is that he missed the chase, and I know how to play the game. And it wasn't hard. All I understood was that his affection meant jewels, and gifts, and money, and attention.

But my uncle had far bigger plans. He knew that Henry wanted to be rid of Anna. He thought he could put another Howard girl in the king's bed—maybe even on the throne. He liked being uncle to the queen. Plus, he needed a spy in court. And if I were to have a boy, he said, we could rival the Seymours and bring Cromwell down once and for all. As family to the heir, he said, the Seymours were getting way too big for their boots. And so this was my uncle's brilliant plan.

In that, my uncle understood Henry well. He had done his time with the dignified Queen Catherine; he had fought like a tiger with the fiery Anne Boleyn; he had deflowered his precious Jane and sent her to the undertaker with her guts hanging out. He was old, reeking, and stuck with a wife who was stupid enough to let him know it. His only heir was a baby in the cradle, and he needed a spare. He just wanted a pliant young body.

He called me a jewel, a rose, a perfect little English maid. He praised my golden hair, my clear skin, my tiny waist. That old man pinched me and prodded me and patted me on the arse. He gave me land, money, diamonds, anything I asked for. My head was turned. And I didn't stop for a second to think. I didn't realise that the men who idealise you like a delicious piece of fruit can become furious and smash you to the wall when you're a little bruised. And I didn't think beyond wanting to be queen. I didn't have a clue what that meant. By then, all I had was my looks and an emptiness inside me.

Besides, he was ancient. I hoped he'd die soon anyway.

Oh, what, you think me callous? Henry chose our wedding day to execute Cromwell. How's that for a celebration?

And no trial, either. Henry had figured out this Bill of Attainder thing, which meant he could be sentenced to death without a trial.

And so, we were married at Oatlands Palace in Surrey. He even chose my motto for me: "No other will but his." That put me right in my place. I might have been married to the king, but I was never, really. All the other lady's maids with whom I'd served Queen Anna never paid me the slightest mind.

 ANNA: *In fairness, Kitty, it did look ridiculous, putting a child on the throne of Queen Catherine.*

Well, that wasn't my problem, was it? I was queen, and they really should have shown me respect. You did, Anna, even though I'd taken your husband. You came back to court, all gracious and lovely, the king's new sister—that confused me a bit—and gave us beautiful gifts.

I suppose she was quite rich, actually. Being the King's Beloved Sister was pretty lucrative. She never made me feel bad. She never chastised me. She even danced with me, when our old husband had to go to bed because his old legs hurt so much.

 ANNA: *Actually, I felt guilty. I knew what I'd doomed you to.*

Well, I liked being queen, I think. At least, everybody said I should. I was rich and free and happy. I wore a different gown of silk, embroidered with gold and pearls, every single day. I was only eighteen, and I had everything a girl could ever want.

I had money. I had clothes. I had little lapdogs that I adored. I had my friends—or servants, anyway. I had my family—or my uncle, that is. I had dancing and attention, and it was *wild*. I had stepchildren—well, sort of. Elizabeth was too small, and the baby was boring. Princess Mary wouldn't lower herself to talk to me, and she kept that title for Anna of Cleves. In fairness, looking back, it must have been *awful* for her. It was one thing for her father to marry Jane Seymour, who apparently he really loved, or Anna of Cleves, a noblewoman with good political connections. In her mind, it was an insult to her mother's memory for Henry to cast off another legitimate wife for a girl like me, five years younger than her. Besides, she was really religious, or something, so I think she thought that Henry was still married to Anna. Which he wasn't, I'm at least 90 percent sure of it.

He was like a god: the most powerful king in the world, and Supreme Head of the Church. He could see all my sins and every bad thing I'd ever done. And he wanted me anyway. So I could have cared for him. I certainly obeyed without question for a while. But here's the story you never heard. He *disgusted* me. He sweated all over me every single night. He tried and tried, and tried again. I had to do all sorts of things to get him hard, things I'd learned for love and never thought I'd have to use on an old man.

And then, the inevitable happened. Come on, what did you expect? I fell in love. And not with Henry, either. One of the grooms of his bedchamber, Thomas Culpeper. He was the most handsome boy at court. He was beautiful. He was dashing. I was desperate, trapped with an old man who didn't do it for me. And Thomas was reckless enough to try.

He was also a rapist. That's something I'll bet you didn't know, either. Yep, my one true love, the man I risked it all for? A rapist. He had grabbed some married woman and held her down in the bushes. When some villagers tried to help, he killed one. He was arrested, and Henry forgave him. So that's who I fell for. And don't judge me too harshly. By that point, I didn't know any better.

ANNE: *But you should have done, cousin Kitty. Look what happened to me, just because of some petty flirtation! You should have learnt from my mistakes.*

Come on, Anne, you did more damage to the family than I ever could have. You were a great queen in their eyes. I was just fresh meat.

ANNE: *There were spies everywhere! Everyone was watching you like a hawk. You might have been a child, but you were Queen of England!*

But Tom didn't treat me like that, you see. He treated me like I was just a young woman, special only to him, but a delicious treat he was prepared to risk his life for.

I wanted it, too. But I needed help. And that's where Lady Jane Rochford came in. Widow to George Boleyn, brother of Anne. She was the one who they say betrayed her husband and her family in order to save her own neck. They say it was her fault that Anne lost hers. But that can't be right. They were family.

Besides, she wanted to help me. And what did it matter to me why? She was our go-between. And she helped us meet in secret, time and time again. Maybe she did it for love of love, who knows?

 ANNE: *And maybe she did it because she was a sick, jealous witch.*

Yeah, well, either way. She got me what I wanted: time alone with Tom. And we did it every single time we could. It was the best sex of my life.

 CATHERINE PARR: *You had a very short life, Kitty. If you'd hung on a bit longer and waited until Henry was dead—as I did—maybe you and Tom could've been happy together.*

You might think that, but you'd be wrong. The king might have been old and limp and costive, but he lived long enough to cause trouble for you, didn't he?

Besides, trouble was coming for me, anyway. Tales of my high jinks at Lambeth were coming to court. Francis Dereham arrived out of nowhere in August, wanting to work in my household. I did warn him not to tell anyone about our past...*indiscretions*, but I was too indiscreet myself. I told one friend; I told another.

And so, in the autumn, when we went on that long-awaited Northern Progress, some woman who was with me at Lambeth talked to her brother about my past. He talked to the Archbishop of Canterbury, Thomas Cranmer. A big rival of my family, staunch Roman Catholics. So *he* told the king, on 2 November—All Soul's Day. They slipped the charge against me into his hand while he was at Mass.

I might have gotten away with my affair. Henry was told only stuff about me from before my marriage. I could have claimed pre-contract with Francis Dereham and been no worse off than Anna of Cleves. But there were too many loose ends, too many witnesses. And they took Francis Dereham to the Tower and tortured him until he confessed—and told them about Tom. And then they took Lady Rochford, and she confessed, too.

There was an investigation, and they found my letter. So that spring, 1541, my husband the king had been really sick. Again. Something to do with his legs? Or a fever. Or infection. Or whatever. But he was always sick, and everybody thought he was going to die. And I did something stupid. I wrote a letter to my beloved Tom, and I *signed my name*.

If you learn only one thing from me, it's this: never put in writing what you wouldn't want your mother to read. And my love letter was pretty loving, despite all the poor spelling and misshapen letters. In fact, I signed it "Yours as long as life endures."

I'd signed my own death warrant, and Tom's, too.

So then they knew that I'd been cheating on the king with Tom while I was married. And Henry's temper exploded. I never saw it, but I heard that his fury, his humiliation, his disappointment were unparalleled.

They stripped me of the queenship and sent me to Syon Abbey and imprisoned me there for the whole winter. Cranmer tormented me into confessing—although I always maintained that Francis and I weren't really betrothed and that he raped me.

And Francis Dereham was hung, drawn, and quartered. My beloved Tom was lucky by comparison—he was beheaded. I comfort myself that at least it was quick.

I was deserted, left to freeze in that old convent. My uncle, the Duke of Norfolk, managed to save his own skin yet again. And nobody came to help. And in February, so I heard, they passed a bill that made it treason for the wife of the king not to disclose any sexual history within twenty days of marriage or to commit adultery. So I was guilty without a trial. Always read your paperwork.

I screamed when the lords came for me the next month. Screamed the walls down. But still nobody helped. They hauled me out onto a barge, and we passed under London

Bridge, where both Francis's and Tom's heads rotted on spikes.

But I didn't scream when they finally organised my execution. I wanted to be composed, collected, queenly. The last time everyone was going to look at me? I didn't want to get it wrong. I had them bring the execution block into my cell. I spent the night practising, kneeling with my cheek on the cold stone, wondering what it would feel like to feel the swish of the ax.

It didn't help. On the day they came for me, I was so paralysed with fear that I could hardly move or speak. I didn't stride to my death like my brave cousin Anne. The same block, same place. They had to haul me up there. At least when the ax came down, it was a clean death. Lady Jane Rochford, the architect of so much trouble, had to put her face on the stone block right after me. But hers was already covered in blood.

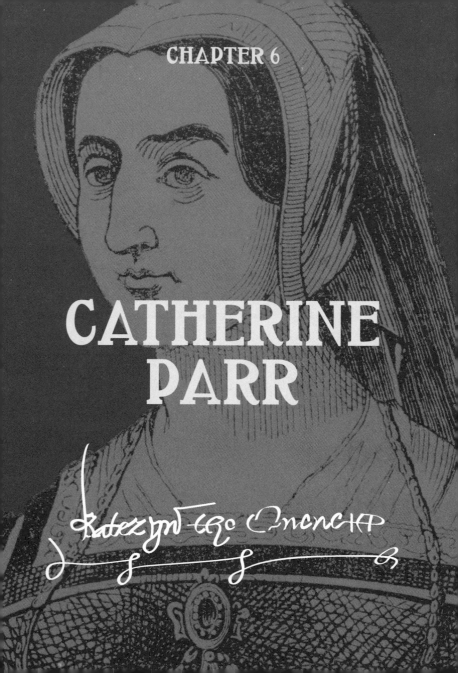

CHAPTER 6

CATHERINE PARR

PROFILE

NAME: Catherine Parr, also known as Katherine, Cateryn, or Cat

OTHER TITLES: Lady Latimer, Regent of England (when Henry went on campaign in France, July–September 1544); Queen Dowager

BORN: August (?) 1512, probably in the Parr Blackfriars townhouse

PARENTS: Sir Thomas Parr, lord of the manor of Kendal in Westmorland (Cumbria), and Maud Green, Northamptonshire heiress

NOTABLE ANCESTORS: King Edward III; Sir Thomas Green, lord of Greens Norton, Northamptonshire

SIBLINGS: William (born 1513), later 1st Marquess of Northampton; Anne (born 1514), later Countess of Pembroke

CHILDHOOD: Father died in 1517; probably grew up in Northamptonshire

LOOKS: Tall, long fair chestnut hair, short nose, stately and poised, characterful face

PERSONALITY: Sensible, scholarly, maternal, straight-talking, glamorous, loved music, dutiful, pious

EDUCATION: Highly literate; fluent in French, Italian, and Latin, and learned some Spanish; scholar of religion and the Bible

RELIGION: Raised a Catholic but became interested in reform and Protestantism

MARRIAGES:

- Edward Borough, son of Thomas, Lord Borough (chamberlain to Queen Anne Boleyn), in 1529, age sixteen; became Lady Borough
- John Neville, Lord Latimer, in 1534; became Lady Latimer
- Henry VIII, on 12 July 1543 at Hampton Court Palace
- Thomas Seymour, in May 1547

AGE DIFFERENCE WITH HENRY: twenty-one years

MOTTO: "To be useful in all I do"

CHILDREN: One, and five stepchildren: two from Lord Latimer; John and Margaret; and three from Henry VIII

- 30 August 1548, a girl, Mary Seymour

MARRIAGE ENDED: When Henry died (28 January 1547)

DIED: 5 September 1548, from childbed fever, age about thirty-six

BURIED: St. Mary's Chapel on Sudeley Castle grounds

DID YOU KNOW?

- Henry's first wife, Catherine of Aragon, was my godmother. I was probably named after her.

- Henry was my third of four husbands, making me the most married of the six.

- I was in love with Thomas Seymour, the brother of Jane Seymour, and wanted to marry him—but duty to the king prevailed.

- I was the first Queen of England to also be Queen of Ireland, after Henry adopted the title.

- I loved greyhounds and parrots and kept both as pets.

- I was one of only eight women to have books published in the sixty years of Henry VII and Henry VIII.

- My book *Prayers or Meditations* (1545) was the first book published in England by a woman under her own name. Ever.

- Before Henry died, he decreed that I should be respected as the queen even after his death.

- After I died, my last husband, Thomas Seymour, tried to marry my stepdaughter, Princess Elizabeth. He was beheaded for treason.

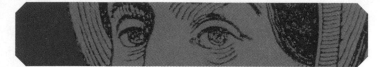

Right, that's it. I've had it up to *here* with all this doom and gloom. So much whining, and for what? Is your marriage to Henry really how you want to define yourself? I lived a full life before I met Henry—and a happy one after he died. Mostly. You've all just spent the last I-don't-know-how-many-pages talking about how your lives led up to Henry.

And so much for "survived." I barely got away from that marriage with my life. But if it's a competition you want, you've got it. If you want to get technical, I was the only one of the six who was queen in my own right, without Henry as my overlord. When he finally died, swollen and rotting and covered in pus, he told the country that they should continue to honour me, until my stepson Edward came to the throne. That makes me the most queenly of all of us.

 JANE: *And who was he buried next to, Mistress Parr?*

Oh, give it a rest, Jane. You bovine bore. You were the wet blanket on my entire marriage. You might have got his corpse, but I knew your husband and your son better than you ever did.

JANE: *And you were his widow for about five minutes before you married my brother.*

Low blow. But you're not wrong. That one did come back to bite me.

KATHERINE: *Plus, he was so devastated after he killed me that he married you only after two years.*

That isn't quite how it happened, Kitty. Besides, it's my turn to talk.

In fairness, Henry *was* devastated after Katherine Howard's death. All his moping and wailing, you'd think he wasn't the monster who killed her. It's not clear whether it really was Katherine he was mourning or the total loss of all five wives. All the grief, the disappointment, the money, the hassle.

But when Katherine Howard died, it was the first time in a long time—maybe all his life—that Henry didn't have the next one ready and waiting in his arms. He needed another wife, to care for his son and, he hoped, provide him with another, but the court was wary. The senseless beheading of that silly child had spooked the lot of them. It was now treason, on pain of death, to suggest that the king marry anyone but the purest of women. It was now treason, on pain of death, not to reveal the sexual past of a would-be queen. A lot of things were treason, on pain of death.

Christ, the *rage* of him. This was not the golden prince of his youth. This was a tyrant, pure and simple. A tyrant who trusted nobody, whom nobody could trust. The king would wake up on the wrong side of the bed and kill someone for it. People were running scared, and nobody knew who to suggest for his next bedfellow. The pain of disappointment in Katherine was too much for him to bear. Some of the greatest families in the land had let him down, putting two bewitching whores in his bed.

But even if a clever courtier could find a match he might go for, would she go for him? A two-time wife-killer? And he wasn't exactly the dashing figure of his youth, either. His rude awakening to himself with Anna of Cleves had taught him that. He was an old man, an ugly man, a scared man, with just a sickly little boy for an heir after all his attempts. And by then, his health was failing rapidly. His weight, already growing steadily since his accident in 1536 that opened up his old jousting wound, was ballooning. He could barely walk and needed to be wheeled around the palaces in a sort of mechanical chair. His appetites were impossible to satisfy. He ate and ate because he could no longer satisfy himself with sex. Yes, that was failing, too.

There were even those ballsy enough—or sufficiently lacking a sense of irony—to suggest that he take Anna of

DON'T L*O*SE YOUR HEAD

Cleves back, the dull German duck who'd so impressed the country with her grace and dignity. Everybody said that the freedom and wealth that came with being his sister, rather than his wife, had let her blossom into nice clothes and good living. But he'd got himself into a bind there, too, because he'd told the whole world she was a smelly, unchaste cow. Plus the fact that he'd told the whole world she was pre-contracted to another man.

He began to look back: to the only wife who'd never disappointed him. The one who had given him what he most wanted—a son. He began to idolise the woman he'd barely known for a second in life. It was the start of Saintly Jane. What woman could live up to the artificial memory of perfection? Such is the lot in life of all women who marry a widower.

I should know. I'd married one myself before. Let me tell you all about it.

I don't remember much about my childhood. My parents were a huge deal in the North, which meant they were a smaller deal in London. But they were close to the crown. My mother, Maud, a great Northamptonshire heiress, was lady-in-waiting to Catherine of Aragon. That's actually where I got my name. It's kind of ironic that I ended up marrying her husband.

My father, Thomas Parr of Kendal, died when I was just a child. He was kind of fourth cousins with Henry, actually, descended from Edward III. My mother, left in the lurch, stayed with the queen. I never studied with Princess Mary, but the other girls at court and I were all taught the lessons of Juan Luis Vives and the humanism he described.

But all that education wasn't for owt when my mother gave me over to my first husband when I was just sixteen. Lord Edward Borough—son of Thomas, who was actually one of Anne Boleyn's chamberlains—was in his twenties but was sickly as anything. My mother had spent all her money on a good marriage for my brother, William, and got only scraps for me. Luckily, he was dead within a year. That left me free as a bird but poor as a beggar. It was the year after my poor mother died, too, so I got to choose my next husband.

And nobody was really sure what I was thinking when I chose John Neville—or Lord Latimer, as he was known. He was in his mid-forties, a widow twice over with two children. I became Lady Latimer and a stepmother to boot. We were married just around the time that Henry was crowning Anne Boleyn queen, but I was a lot more successful than her. My husband taught me how to run a house, how to manage a fortune, how to act like a mother to his two children— everything, basically, that would stand me in good stead as soon as he upped and died.

But before that came the Pilgrimage of Grace, in 1536. Those Northern Catholic rebels rose up against Henry and all that he'd done to make a Church of England. They

DON'T L*O*SE YOUR HEAD

hated Cromwell and the dissolution of the monasteries. They hated the closure of the abbeys. They hated Henry for throwing off Catherine of Aragon and beheading Anne Boleyn. Eventually, nearly forty thousand men marched on Lincoln and ended up squatting in the Cathedral.

They dragged my husband away, trying to force him to help build a metaphorical bridge between England and Rome. I never forgave them for that, as I was left to cower with his children.

Latimer left me to protect his home, his children, his house. And when the uprising hit the gates of his Snape Castle in Yorkshire, they took *us* hostage and put us under house arrest, and he had to run straight back up North. They threatened to kill us all.

Latimer managed to talk those Catholics out of doing anything stupid, but he later had to ride down south in shame to explain that he'd been forced to go along with them. The only reason he even got away with it was that my brother intervened with the king.

That was sort of it for me and the North, though. Down south we went, to my London house in Charterhouse Yard. Things improved some after Cromwell died, and my husband started to visit Parliament.

My sister Anne—we called her Nan—had done quite well for herself, marrying William Herbert (illegitimate grandson to the Earl of Pembroke) and getting her claws in at court as part of the new Reformist movement. That was in the time of Queen Jane Seymour, Queen Anna of Cleves, and Queen Katherine Howard, one right after the other, and my sister had served them all.

My husband was dying. But he was dying for a really bloody long time. I nursed him for almost a year.

And so I came to court to visit. And that was when I fell in love.

It was where I met Thomas Seymour—Tom, as I knew him. I hate to talk in clichés, but he was the first and only man I ever truly wanted to marry. He was the brother of Jane Seymour, and full of himself, too. Handsome, charming, passionate, absolutely *insatiable* in the sack—if the rumours were true, that is. He was up and coming, for sure, and he started courting me the moment Lord Latimer finally shuffled off this mortal coil. I don't think it hurt that I was a very wealthy widow. Plus, I had been married to one young weakling and one old invalid, and I was ready for love. And so we decided to marry.

But the king wasn't immune to me, either. And when poor little Katherine Howard put her head on the block because she couldn't keep her legs shut, everything changed. Henry had started sending me gifts while my husband was still dying. And I was suddenly a deer in his sights, too.

So why me? Why did the old king come sniffing about me, a sensible (mostly) widow of thirty-one? I might have had a tiny drop of royal blood (I think we were third cousins or something?), but I was hardly an obvious prospect. I was no great beauty or dazzling flirt: I was just a sensible Northern widow with no room for guff. I was tall and fair and liked to strut around the dance floor in jewelled clothes and finery, but that was my only indulgence in silliness.

But as I said, I was no spring chicken, and I'd never managed to have any children in either of my marriages. So what was in it for him? I wasn't the clear choice to give him more heirs. Maybe that was it. You must know by now that his manhood had almost completely failed him. Getting together with a barren woman would hide the fact that it was his plumbing that didn't work. The talk had moved away from him having another child to him marrying off Princess Mary to a suitable man.

But he was old, and scared, and sick. He didn't need a silly child like Kitty Howard anymore. He didn't need a fixer-upper like Anna of Cleves or another great love like Jane or Anne. What he needed was a helper. He needed a nurse, a scholar. That's where I came in. And hey, the money didn't hurt, either.

But can you actually believe it, even after all that time there were *still* people pushing him back toward dumpy Anna of Cleves. There were still rumours about her, you know, even though she stopped coming to court after Katherine Howard was executed. People said she'd had Henry's child. People said she'd had someone *else's* child. Of course, it was all utter codswallop, but people said it.

Meanwhile, the Cleves people were pushing the idea, as you can imagine. And Anna was, to put it lightly, *uneager*.

 ANNA: *Na ja, are you crazy? You think I was going back to that court after he cut off a child's head? And he liked her more than me!*

Hardly. He actually got pretty fond of you, as his sister. And you could've been a bit friendlier, by the way. All you did was sneer at the "burden" I'd taken upon myself. But I knew what I was getting myself into far better than you did. I wasn't some dumb Dutch peasant; I was a seasoned widow with a mind of steel.

 ANNA: *It was an insult. Even more than when he married Kitty. It was a final scorn.*

I did learn from you, though. You know what, I learnt from all the wives. I was as scholarly minded as Catherine of Aragon. I was obedient like Jane Seymour. I was maternal like Anna of Cleves. I was passionately committed to reform, just like Anne Boleyn. And I lost my head over a Thomas, just like Katherine Howard.

 KATHERINE: *Er, not literally, you didn't. Mind your manners.*

But Henry was having none of it. And he got rid of my Thomas by sending him off to the Netherlands. And when he proposed, I had a choice to make.

So the thing you need to know about me is I was kind of pious. I might have been raised a Catholic, but I'd become as interested in Protestantism and reform as any smart, young self-taught woman at court. And as far as I was concerned, Henry could be the defender of the faith that had taken us *away* from the hefty corruption of Rome. Nan and my brother-in-law urged me to accept, for the sake of the country's future. You see, this is why sex and religion shouldn't mix.

I didn't want to marry Henry—seriously, would you have wanted to? But I did feel, pretty strongly, that I had to. It was almost like a vocation, a calling to a duty. I thought I could lead him away from the Pope and further toward reform. I should have known that you couldn't lead Henry anywhere that wasn't by his ego, stomach, or cock.

I let duty take charge over love, and I knew I'd be rewarded in the long run. I thought I was going along with God's will, but since when did God ever care about a young woman's sexual preference? I don't know if Thomas and I could've escaped—if I'd even had a choice at all—but either way, I said yes. I gave up my own personal passions and desires because I really wanted to make the country better. Thomas let me go, and Nan and I stepped up to the plate.

It was a small, quiet wedding. My third, his sixth, so no need for a big fuss. Henry and I got hitched on 12 July in the queen's closet at Hampton Court Palace, where he'd married Jane and Anna. But unlike them, I became Queen of Ireland as well as of England because Henry had grabbed that, too.

DID YOU KNOW?

Mine was the first Protestant funeral in England, Scotland, or Ireland to be conducted in English.

The painting of me in the National Portrait Gallery was thought for a long time to be of Lady Jane Grey—she was the granddaughter of Henry's sister.

In 1792, some drunken fools opened my coffin and reburied me upside down.

I chose for my motto "To be useful in all I do." And do you know something? That's really what I tried.

Right off the bat, I wanted to be a good stepmother. Princess Mary, who had suffered so much with her father's changeable nature, was about twenty-six then: it was a good age to marry, and she would make a great heiress if Henry didn't change his mind again. He seemed a lot closer to her than he ever had before, letting her take centre stage at feasts as if she were a little queen herself. She and I shared a connection—my mother, Maud, had been devoted to Queen Catherine—so there was some warmth between us.

Elizabeth was just a precocious poppet of nine. The two girls had at last had a bit of luck, though, in the summer when a new Succession Act put them at the back of the line to the throne after Edward. The prince was still a little noble imp in short clothes, but Henry was already scheming to get him betrothed to Mary, Queen of Scots. They all needed a mother because Henry saw them as pawns.

I put a lot of time, effort, and energy into reconciling him with his two daughters. I know it's a process that Anna of Cleves began—yes, Anna, we know—but I saw it through. The royal children became my children, just by default because I didn't have any others. I also continued to care for my stepson and stepdaughter from my last marriage and put them in high places at court.

My brother, William Parr, who had so often stolen the limelight of attention—and money—when Nan and I were growing up was suddenly massively indebted to us both as he used my new position to advance himself. He became Baron Parr and a Knight of the Garter. Luckily, he was also a lot nicer than he had been as a snot-nosed kid. He was friendly and charming to everyone. Between his popularity and Nan's expertise on queens, I managed to pull it off. I hid my passion and became subservient, dutiful, *submissive*.

But I'll not lie to you, it was strange being the sixth wife. I inherited *so much* from the previous wives, you know. Their clothes, their heels, their hoods, their jewels, even their perfumes. Even Katherine Howard's precious sables. Because of that, I spent a *fortune* on new clothes and jewels. People thought I was a magpie, but really it was just a sensible way to distance myself from the past.

And there were other, less palatable parts of being queen. Just like my previous husband, Henry needed a lot of nursing. His leg was causing him agony, and he could barely stand. They bled him, they leeched him, they cut his leg open and held it there by stuffing it with gold chips. The doctors and quack apothecaries tried everything. But it was clear that Henry was a very sick man. So I moved into a tiny room next door to help him, even though it meant that more often than not I had to get into his bed, and try and make him do what he hadn't managed with at least one of his previous wives.

Jesus, it was horrible. Sometimes doing your duty makes you gag.

So I threw myself into education. I taught myself Latin—Edward, bless his socks, used to write to me and correct my grammar. I tried Italian so that Elizabeth could write to me in that, too, but I struggled a lot. Mary, as highly educated as a scholar, helped me. I like to think that in those hours we spent together, some of her mother's influence, my godmother, Catherine of Aragon, rubbed off on me.

 CATHERINE OF ARAGON: *You have no idea.*

Really? God, I'm glad you think so. Because I was called upon to be regent, just like you were, and I think we did it kind of differently.

Because it was 1544, and Henry was off to war with France again. And the Scots, being Scots, were making trouble again. Although he never had me crowned, Henry made it understood that I was in charge while he was gone. And off he went, on that mechanical contraption that lifted him up onto his stalwart horse, with his bad leg horribly swollen.

Still, when I wrote to Henry as regent, it was with none of Catherine of Aragon's respectful but firm dominance. And I might not have literally rallied the troops into battle as she had done, but I did sign a lot of important papers, which is more than any of the other wives since her ever did. I organised the finances for his army, and everyone who's ever been in war knows how important that is. I was basically in charge of the kingdom. As I said to Princess Elizabeth, who watched me closely as if she could read her future in my face, "If a woman can read and teach herself, there's no reason why she can't do anything a man does. Better, probably."

I carried on airily: "You should always be able to outsmart your man." But, I quickly added, "It is inadvisable for him to know this."

But Scotland didn't want to play ball—it never did. Their parliament rejected our treaty, rejected the idea of a marriage between Prince Edward and Mary, Queen of Scots, and rejected us, the English. Edward Seymour, Prince Edward's uncle and Jane's brother, attacked southern Scotland right back for that. And so began the "rough wooing of Scotland."

Those were tough times for the country but especially for its finances. All that money that Henry had taken from the monasteries was poured into the ridiculous hollow fight with France, while I tried to hold the fort at home against Scotland with less and less.

To pull off being regent, I got close with Archbishop Thomas Cranmer—my uncle, actually. We talked more and more about God, and religion, and the Bible, and the sweeping reforms that Henry had wrought on the country. Yes, I'd been brought up a Catholic, but between my sister and the mood of the court I became more and more interested in the new ways. After all, Catholicism was full of a lot of *silliness*. I kept saying to my stepdaughter, Princess Mary, "You're surely not telling me you *really*, *literally* believe in transubstantiation? That the wafer and wine *literally* turn into the body of Christ during Mass?"

(She did. But we carried on debating it anyway.)

I became great friends with Katherine, the Duchess of Suffolk. She was actually the daughter of María de Salinas, and she had the sharpest mind in the kingdom. Seven years younger than me and running around my arguments. We had more fun than you might think debating the Bible.

So all that was how I ended up writing my first book. It wasn't anything glamorous—just a translation of some prayers. It didn't even rile my husband, who by those days was getting riled by anything and everything. You could look at him funny after luncheon and find yourself in the Tower by dinner. Those were scary days, but there was something about those simple little prayers that called to me. I was missing my Thomas, unsatisfied by my marriage, and nervous about my position, but at least I had my book.

It was anonymous, obviously, but word soon got out. And Bishop Stephen Gardiner and Lord Chancellor Thomas

Wriothesley were none too happy about the queen sympathising with the so-called Protestant cause.

When I wrote my first proper book, *Prayers or Meditations*, in 1545, they nearly went apeshit. I based it on a Catholic book, *The Imitation of Christ*, but rejigged it for the new Church of England. It was the first book ever published in England, in English, under a woman's own name.

I had Cranmer's permission, and I had my husband's, and I was proud as a puffed-up rooster when it came out. And, do you know what, *people liked it*. Elizabeth sat up and took notice of how a woman could use her brain to become powerful. She was still just a child, but she translated that book into Italian, French, and Latin as a gift for Henry. I even encouraged Reformer thought in the baby court of Prince Edward.

Probably the most important person in my intellectual journey was Anne Askew, the great martyr. I was completely *obsessed* with her. She, a devout Protestant, had been married off to a Catholic pig who beat her every chance he got. She tried to divorce him, and he threw her out. So the newly single, free woman came to London to preach the gospel of Protestantism. She even came to lecture at my little Bible studies group. But Wriothesley and Gardiner feared what they didn't understand: independent, intellectual women.

The bishops cross-examined that girl for heresy, and when she wouldn't admit any fault, they became enraged and tortured her themselves. And still she wouldn't say a word against me, which is what they really wanted. They racked her until she was broken into a thousand pieces. It even shocked the guards. And when she was so crippled that she couldn't move, they burned her for heresy. She died a martyr to the Protestant cause, but really she died to save me.

Then those two old demons still tried to turn Henry against me; they tried to have me arrested. I saw a copy of the warrant. But I got wind of their plot and managed to talk Henry 'round. I don't really want to remember what I had to do to earn his forgiveness. Let's just say prayer isn't the only useful thing you can do on your knees. I promised never to presume to argue with him, or have an opinion, again.

Those were very dark days, those last days of Henry's life. You never knew where you stood with him, so most of the time it was better to leave him be: to bite your tongue. Nobody ever got anywhere by backchatting a man in pain. He was burning heretics left, right, and centre, and nobody knew what they should and shouldn't believe. The whole drama hinged on whether or not the common people should be allowed to read the Bible themselves, in English. To me, it seemed a no-brainer. But I never said a word.

How, *how* Jane Seymour managed to keep the title of Protestant queen instead of me I'll never understand. But she hung over my marriage in other, more tangible ways— like when Henry commissioned a massive portrait of us with his children, a family picture. A spectacular work of art that would echo through the ages and show our descendants what we were about. A portrait that was a snapshot of everything I'd given up and everything I'd taken on. There were my shoes, my clothes I'd so carefully picked that day, my body that I'd held so still for the painter. And then there was Jane Seymour's stiff white face.

I was the one who wrote to her son. I was the one whom Edward called "my dearest mother." I was the one who nursed Henry through his last days, the one who gave up my true love and my freedom for the sake of the cause. And it was her face, not mine, that ended up immortalised.

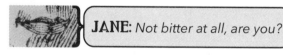 **JANE:** *Not bitter at all, are you?*

Not especially. Besides, it was my funeral that was the first Protestant service held in English. So.

But religious disagreements were all swept aside when the last of Henry's strength began to fail him. That Christmas, 1546, he was shut up in his rooms most of the time. He sent my ladies and me away to celebrate at Greenwich while he stayed to rest in London. I never saw him again. He didn't say goodbye to me, either.

Who knows what really went on in those last days, how the men of the court moved to secure their own influence? How the Seymour family swooped in to protect their great heir, Prince Edward? None of us knows for sure.

What we do know is that Henry died slowly, in huge pain. It wasn't a noble end to a great king. He was prostrate, rotting from his leg inwards. A stinking, groaning, miserable beast; the greatest Renaissance man could barely speak. The man who'd freed us from the yoke of Rome, who'd lived his life with such unflagging passion. You wouldn't have let a dog die like that. Whatever he'd done to me, whatever he'd done to any of us, he didn't deserve an end like that.

KATHERINE AND ANNE:
Disagree.

Regardless. On 28 January, on his father's birthday, he finally died. The long reign of Henry VIII was over. I watched as they opened up Jane's tomb and laid his massive bulk to rest alongside her, the wife he had so convinced himself he loved. And I thought, Now I'm free to do what I want.

Everybody jumped as soon as his pulse stopped. Edward Seymour, uncle to the new King Edward, managed to make himself Protector of the Kingdom—despite the fact that Henry's will had clearly appointed sixteen equal regents. I wasn't one of the regents, by the way.

By the time Edward was crowned, I'd already retired from court to my home in Chelsea. I wanted no more of it. But I was an even richer widow than before. And Thomas, my beloved, his equally ambitious brother, hurried back to court as well. He was made 1st Baron of Sudeley, and he still wanted to marry me. Because there I was, first lady of the land, Dowager Queen, and dripping with jewels. I can't imagine that hurt.

But it wasn't just about the money and the power, you know. Our connection was so powerful that, even by forty, he'd never married or wanted another woman. And, God help me, I still wanted him, too. He came to visit me at night in my gardens. And by May, he was back in bed.

I knew they would never agree to the Dowager Queen, the widow of the king, remarrying so soon. But I'd spent my whole life doing what I thought was right for others. I wanted to be selfish for once.

We married in secret, but the scandal got out eventually. What the *hell* was I thinking? I look back after all this time and I'm astonished at my own wild recklessness. Maybe I had more in common with Katherine Howard after all.

Prince Edward, now King Edward VI, was hurt and confused. Thomas and I wrote to Mary for help, but she was disgusted with me and turned her back on us both. She even told Elizabeth, my little ward, to do the same. And Edward Seymour, the Protector, was enraged.

So even as my relationship with my stepchildren went to hell, so too did Thomas's with his brother. Edward, now 1st Duke of Somerset, was married to this shrew Anne Seymour—my former lady-in-waiting. She said that I couldn't wear the queen's jewels, as was my right as Dowager Queen, and that she should be allowed to wear them as the wife of the Protector. She won, and got my jewels. Edward even kept my wedding ring. Thomas took it as a huge insult.

I did feel safe enough to publish my last book, *Lamentation of a Sinner*, which was *overtly* anti-Rome and pro-Protestant. I heard Mary wasn't best pleased about the anti-Rome bit, but she wasn't talking to me by then, anyway. I didn't really care because something incredible had happened. I was pregnant. After all those long, barren years, I'd finally conceived a child, with the love of my life.

And then, you know the rest. Princess Elizabeth, my beloved ward, whom I'd treated like a daughter, was a gorgeous, ripe young girl of fifteen. And my husband, Thomas, might have been my beloved, but he was a weak, lustful man like any other. He began to play with her even when I was carrying his baby. He crept in and out of her bedroom, trapping her when she was half naked. He held her down and grabbed her by the legs, on the arse, all over. I tried to look away, I tried to ignore it, but eventually it all got out of control. I had to send her away.

She wrote and told me she was sorry, but I never saw her again. So I lost my Elizabeth, too.

Was it worth it, all the pain I caused? All those years of doing the right thing, of dutiful behaviour and good maternal standards, all tossed because I still had that much physical passion for a man who would grope my stepchild in my own house?

That August, I gave birth to my only child, named Mary Seymour after my estranged stepdaughter, whom I never stopped loving. And just like Jane, the sister-in-law I never met, and so many women before us, I fell into a fever. And although I raged and ranted and screamed betrayal, in the end I forgave Thomas. I forgave Elizabeth. I forgave Henry. I forgave them all. And that's how, six days later, I managed to die in peace.

THE SIX:
A CURTAIN CALL

(AS TOLD BY PRINCESS MARY
AND PRINCESS ELIZABETH)

Marye the quene

Mary Tudor: I did forgive her, you know. When I lost my own head over Philip II of Spain, the swarthy Spaniard I ended up marrying, I understood what Catherine Parr had done, and why. And I never forgot that it was she, and Jane, and Anna of Cleves, who together had pushed my father to reinstate me as his heir. I would never have been queen without them. They didn't stand to gain anything from that.

But this story doesn't end with these six women. After all, the longed-for heir wasn't long on the throne. My little brother, the great Tudor heir, the source of so much joy and conflict and hope and struggle, died of tuberculosis just a few years into his reign.

Elizabeth and I, Henry's unwanted, neglected, beloved bastards, became far more important than he ever could have dreamed. My mother's legacy: that there is no great country where women do not lead.

And when it was my turn for a coronation in 1553, it was Anna of Cleves who led me to Whitehall Palace. And it was her association with Elizabeth that led to her downfall.

It's easy enough now to judge the behaviour of my father's six wives, their choices, and their mistakes. But would any of us have done any better? I doubt it.

Elizabeth: After all, it was Katherine Howard's recklessness with Thomas Culpeper that inspired my wild affair with Robert Dudley. It was Catherine Parr who taught me that a woman could rule with the stomach of the prince. I was sorry for what I'd done to her, too.

The battle between Catherine of Aragon and my mother, Anne Boleyn, played out again between Mary and me. Mary, the beloved child of a great queen, and me, the unwanted daughter of a beheaded whore. And, like my mother, I won.

I watched and waited for my moment with unparalleled nerve and tenacity. Elizabeth II, the last of the Tudor monarchs and the great king my father never was. The princess who was never meant to be queen. And when I ruled, I made sure they re-remembered my mother as the hero of the English reformation that she always was.

You can trace the legacy of all six of my father's wives, down through their children and stepchildren, to another princess who was never meant to be queen: Elizabeth I, the longest-reigning monarch in British history. So in a way, they all survived.

THE SIX: A CURTAIN CALL

TIMELINE

⇢ 1485 ⇠

- 🌐 **22 August:** The Battle of Bosworth Field, in which Richard III is killed, marks the end of the Wars of the Roses
- 🌐 **16 December:** Catherine of Aragon is born

⇢ 1491 ⇠

- 🌐 **28 June:** Henry VIII is born

⇢ 1499 ⇠

- 🌐 **19 May:** Catherine of Aragon marries Prince Arthur by proxy

⇢ 1501 ⇠

- 🌐 **17 August:** Catherine of Aragon leaves Spain forever
- 🌐 **November:** Catherine of Aragon marries Arthur for real
- 🌐 Anne Boleyn is (probably) born

⇢ 1502 ⇠

- 🌐 Arthur dies
- 🌐 **October:** Henry becomes Duke of Cornwall

⇢ 1503 ⇠

- 🌐 **February:** Henry becomes new Prince of Wales

- 🌐 **11 February:** Elizabeth of York, Henry VIII's mother, dies
- 🌐 **23 June:** Marriage treaty is signed between Henry VIII and Catherine of Aragon

⇢ 1504 ⇠

- 🌐 **26 November:** Isabella I of Castile dies

⇢ 1509 ⇠

- 🌐 Jane Seymour is (probably) born
- 🌐 **21 April:** Henry's father, Henry VII, dies; Henry becomes king, declares he will marry Catherine of Aragon
- 🌐 **11 June:** Henry VIII and Catherine of Aragon are married
- 🌐 **24 June (Midsummer Day):** Henry VIII and Catherine of Aragon are crowned
- 🌐 **29 June:** Margaret Beaufort, Henry's grandmother, dies
- 🌐 **August:** Catherine of Aragon announces her first pregnancy

⇢ 1510 ⇠

- 🌐 **31 January:** Catherine of Aragon delivers her first child, a stillborn girl

DON'T LOSE YOUR HEAD

⊕ **May:** Catherine of Aragon announces her second pregnancy

→ 1511 ←

⊕ **1 January:** Henry and Catherine's son is born: Henry, Duke of Cornwall

⊕ **22 February:** Henry and Catherine's son dies, possibly of intestinal problems

→ 1512 ←

⊕ Catherine Parr is (probably) born

→ 1513 ←

⊕ **11 June:** Henry makes Catherine regent

⊕ **30 June:** Henry invades France and defeats the French army at the Battle of the Spurs

⊕ **9 September:** Catherine, heavily pregnant, leads the army and defeats the Scots

⊕ **17 September:** Catherine gives birth to a son prematurely; he dies soon after

⊕ Anne Boleyn is sent to Burgundy

→ 1514 ←

⊕ Henry has bankrupted England

⊕ **June:** Catherine announces her fourth pregnancy

⊕ **November:** Catherine gives birth to another son, who dies soon after

→ 1515 ←

⊕ **Summer:** Catherine announces her fifth pregnancy

⊕ Anna of Cleves is born

→ 1516 ←

⊕ **18 February:** Catherine gives birth to Mary, her only surviving child

⊕ Henry begins an affair with Elizabeth "Bessie" Blount

→ 1518 ←

⊕ **July:** Catherine announces her last pregnancy

⊕ **10 November:** Catherine gives birth for the last time, to a premature daughter who dies soon after

→ 1519 ←

⊕ **15 June:** Bessie Blount gives birth to Henry's illegitimate son, Henry Fitzroy

→ 1520 ←

⊕ Holy Roman Emperor Charles V comes to England to ask for an alliance

 7 June: Henry meets Francis I at the Field of the Cloth of Gold, near Calais (two weeks)

1521

🌐 Charles takes the empire into war with France

1522

🌐 Anne Boleyn arrives in England

1523

🌐 Katherine Howard is born

1527

🌐 **6 May:** Emperor Charles V sacks Rome

🌐 **17 May:** Thomas, Cardinal Wolsey (as papal legate), sets up a secret court and charges the king for living in sin with his brother's widow

🌐 **May:** Henry asks Pope Clement VII to annul his marriage to Catherine

🌐 Henry tells Catherine their marriage is invalid

1528

🌐 **July:** Outbreak of sweating sickness occurs; Anne nearly dies

1529

🌐 **18 June:** The trial begins in Blackfriars

🌐 **October:** Wolsey is charged with praemunire (appealing to foreign authority) and dismissed

1530

🌐 **4 November:** Cardinal Wolsey is charged with treason, dies while waiting for his trial

1532

🌐 **May:** Thomas More resigns as lord chancellor; Thomas Cromwell is chief minister

🌐 **14 November:** Henry and Anne Boleyn marry secretly

1533

🌐 **25 January:** Henry officially marries Anne Boleyn

🌐 **23 May:** Thomas Cranmer convenes court and declares Henry's marriage to Catherine of Aragon void

🌐 **28 May:** Cranmer declares Henry's marriage to Anne Boleyn valid; Catherine is made princess dowager

🌐 **1 June:** Anne is crowned queen

🌐 **11 July:** Pope excommunicates Henry

🌐 **7 September:** Anne Boleyn gives birth to Princess Elizabeth

1534

🌐 **March:** Act of Succession 1533 is passed, declaring Catherine's daughter illegitimate

- Acts of Supremacy recognize the king as head of the church in England

- **Summer:** Anne Boleyn has a false pregnancy or miscarriage

→ 1536 ←

- **7 January:** Catherine of Aragon dies

- **29 January:** Anne Boleyn miscarries a son four months into her pregnancy, on the day of Catherine's funeral

- **January:** Henry falls from his horse in a jousting tournament, reopening an old injury in his leg

- **February:** Dissolution of the Lesser Monasteries Act is passed

- **February:** Henry starts to go after Jane Seymour

- **April:** Anne Boleyn is investigated for high treason

- **May:** Five men are arrested, including Anne Boleyn's brother George; Anne is arrested and sent to the Tower of London, convicted of high treason and adultery; Cranmer annuls Anne's marriage

- **19 May:** Anne Boleyn is executed

- **20 May:** Henry is engaged to Jane Seymour

- **30 May:** Henry and Jane Seymour are married at the Palace of Whitehall, London

- **July:** Henry Fitzroy, Duke of Richmond, dies

- **October:** Pilgrimage of Grace uprising begins in the North

- Second Succession Act declares both Mary and Elizabeth illegitimate

→ 1537 ←

- **12 October:** Jane Seymour gives birth to Prince Edward, future King Edward VI

- **24 October:** Jane Seymour dies of an infection

→ 1538 ←

- **17 December:** Pope Paul III excommunicates Henry VII again

→ 1539 ←

- **January:** Charles and Francis make peace; Charles makes a secret alliance with the emperor

- **27 December:** Anna of Cleves arrives in England

→ 1540 ←

- **January:** Henry meets Anna of Cleves at Rochester Abbey, marries her at the Palace of Placentia

- **24 June:** Henry tells Anna of Cleves to leave the court

9 July: Henry annuls his marriage to Anna of Cleves

28 July: Cromwell is executed; Henry marries Katherine Howard in Oatlands Palace

÷ 1541 ÷

Spring: Katherine Howard meets with Thomas Culpeper; her letter is found

2 November (All Soul's Day): Henry receives a letter in the Chapel Royal about Catherine

7 November: Archbishop Thomas Cranmer and some councilors question Catherine at Winchester Palace

23 November: Katherine is stripped of her title as queen and imprisoned in Syon Abbey

1 December: Thomas Culpeper and Francis Dereham are executed for high treason

÷ 1542 ÷

13 February: Katherine Howard is beheaded

÷ 1543 ÷

12 July: Henry marries Catherine Parr in Hampton Court Palace

Third Succession Act puts the girls back in line to the throne after Edward

÷ 1544 ÷

June: Henry invades France (again) and bankrupts England (again)

÷ 1545 ÷

Warrant is issued for Catherine Parr's arrest

÷ 1547 ÷

28 January: Henry dies in the Palace of Whitehall, on his father's birthday

Prince Edward is crowned King Edward VI

÷ 1548 ÷

5 September: Catherine Parr dies in childbirth

÷ 1553 ÷

6 July: King Edward VI (formerly Prince Edward) dies

Princess Mary is crowned Queen Mary I

÷ 1557 ÷

16 July: Anna of Cleves dies, probably of cancer

DON'T LOSE YOUR HEAD

ACKNOWLEDGMENTS

I may never write another book, so I'd better thank everyone now or I'll never hear the end of it.

First and foremost is my mother, who taught me how to read and write and file a tax return. More or less everything I've done since is therefore her fault. If you don't like this book, please take it up with her. And more power to you.

I signed a book deal right around the time the world stopped: when a coronavirus hijacked the airwaves and slithered across the Channel. Writing at the best of times isn't pretty, much less when you're locked inside like a murderous hog and you're running out of wine. So all hail my flatmate, the propitiously named Catherine, who stood witness to the Jackson Pollocking of my creativity and did most of the cooking.

It is no exaggeration to say that there would be no book without the No.1 Freelance Media Women Facebook group, which posted the commission, and my Awesome Women WhatsApp cartel, who bolstered me with the cojones I needed to pitch for it. As the Fisties say, WWJED? Big shout-out to Sirena Bergman for not canceling me. Yet.

There's also no book without long reads without *The Independent*'s Linda Taylor and Hannah Twiggs: two badass blonde bitches who inexplicably give me endless chances when I've never deserved even one.

A royal debt is due to Casie Vogel of Ulysses Press for her kindness and endless patience.

Rosie Fetherstonhaugh, my local legal eagle, translated my contract into English. Without her, there'd be no cash, so I owe her at least three London rounds.

There were some dark days of the pandemic when the only thing that got me out of bed was Natasha Oakley. For that, she gets my eternal gratitude.

If you're very, very lucky, there'll be one person who steps up when it all goes to shit. For me, that was Roisin Savage. Without her, this book would be a tweet.

My grandmothers, Rhoda and Greta, both taught me in their own indomitable ways how a woman can rule. If I fall even a little short of their example, I will consider myself a success.

For their meticulous research, rich imagination, and passionate dedication, I owe everything to Philippa Gregory, Antonia Fraser, Karen Lindsay, Alison Weir, and Sarah-Beth Watkins. Any and every mistake is mine.

If you've been paying attention, you'll notice that so far I've thanked only women, if only to honor my conviction that we should always come first. That said, there is a damn fine group of men to thank.

A lot of this was written in my head while doggy-paddling in the Royal Docks of London, shivering in a sparkly costume and getting lapped by wet-suited buffoons. For that, I have my old pal Jack Spence to thank.

Without Tim Shipman and Matt d'Ancona, my mentors and longtime idols, I would never have been a journalist. Without Stephen Manning and Zak Thomas, my subeditor inspirations, I would probably have been a waitress.

An unholy amount of Diet Cokes were consumed in the making of this book, bought and hand-delivered by Mark Rofe. He kept me in sunflowers and smiles and made sure that I left the house.

My grandfather Arnold, with his boundless generosity and no small willpower, gave me the space that let me pursue what I most loved: tasteless interior design. And writing.

When your whole shtick is being an "independent woman," it can be awkward to ask for help from a man. Luckily, best friend trumps bloke, and I got the best of both in Jeremy Brown. He practically carried me through a pandemic. I promise to do better in the next one.

Last, but not at all least, I'd like to thank my father, who always said I'd write a book. He's usually right about things (although I'd never admit it on record).

ABOUT THE AUTHOR

Harriet Marsden is a freelance journalist and editor. Previously a subeditor at *The Times*, she now works for a variety of publications, including *The Independent, HuffPost*, the *Guardian*, and *Foreign Policy*. Harriet can often be heard on the radio at stupid o'clock, reviewing the news and mocking politicians. She is also a feminist commentator and contributing author to DK's *The Feminism Book*. Hobbies include reading, swimming, and Broadway musicals (she can do all the raps from *Hamilton*). Harriet has a bachelor's in languages from the University of Cambridge and a master's in international journalism from City University, London. She lives in South London with a cat, two birds, and innumerable plants. This is her first novel.

Harriet can be found tweeting at @harriet1marsden.